THE LAST DAYS OF LORD BUDDHA

With the famous
Sukhavati Vyuha,
The Land of Bliss,
a picture of Buddhist
heaven

Rendered into easy-to-understand English
by the celebrated
Buddhist scholar
T.W. Rhys Davids

Source: *The Book of Great Decease:*
Mahaparinibbana Sutta, Translated by
T.W. Rhys Davids, and The Land of Bliss,
Translated by F. Max Muller, Scred Books
of the East, Vol. II and 49, Oxford University Press,
1894

The Last Days of Lord Buddha
with **The Land of Bliss**

First Edition—2020, **Reprint**—2026
ISBN: 978-81-8383-240-9 (P/B)

Published by:
Lotus Press Publishers & Distributors
4735/22, Prakash Deep Building,
Ansari Road, Darya Ganj, New Delhi-110002
Ph.: 41325510, 9811838000
E-mail: lotuspress1984@gmail.com
www.lotuspress.co.in

Printed & Published: **Lotus Press Publishers & Distributors, New Delhi**

INDIA BOOKVARSITY

LOTUS CHOICES

Editor: Mahendra Kulasrestha

The Last Days of Lord Buddha

The First Prophet of Peace

Mahaparinibbana Sutta

Translated by T.W. Rhys Davids

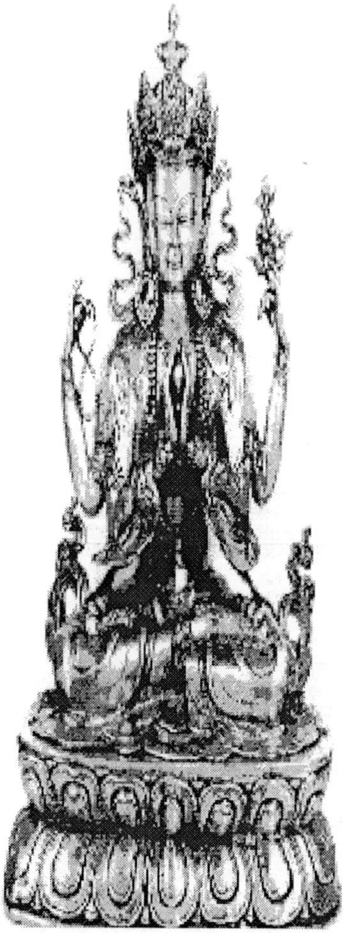

The strangely moving story where you live and move with The Great Ancient Lord

Drawings based on Ajanta Paintings by Reliable Infomedia

4735/22, Ansari Road,
Dary Ganj, New Delhi-110002

Buddhism, the Marvellous

– VIVEKANANDA

Buddhism is historically the most important religion because it was the most tremendous movement the world ever saw, the most gigantic spiritual wave ever to burst upon human society. **There is no civilisation on which its effect has not been felt in some way or the other.**

The followers of Buddha were most enthusiastic and very missionary in spirit. They were the first not to remain content with the limited sphere of their mother church. They travelled east and west, north and south. They went into Persia, Asia Minor, Russia, Poland,...China, Korea, Japan,.. Burma, Siam and beyond.

The civilisation of India has died and revived several times. This is its peculiarity. At the time Buddha was born, India was in need of a great spiritual leader. There was a most powerful body of priests... The Brahmins began to arrogate powers and privileges to themselves. If a Brahmin killed a man, he would not be punished, even the most wicked Brahmin must be worshipped ....two thousand ceremonies they had invented. India was full of it in Buddha's day.

At last one man could bear it no more. He had the brain, the power and the heart—a heart as infinite as the broad sky. He learnt why men suffer, and he found the way out of suffering. **Buddha was the first great preacher of equality.** Every man and woman had the same right to attain spirituality, he opened the door of Nirvana to one and all, even the lowest were entitled to highest attainment. His teaching was bold even for India.

The religion of Buddha spread fast. It was because of the marvellous love which, for the first time in the history of humanity, devoted itself to the service not only of all men but of all living things.

Buddha's idea is that **there is no God, only man himself.** He repudiated the mentality which underlies the prevalent ideas of God. He found it made men weak and superstitious. Everything independent is happy, everything dependent is miserable.

All my life I've been very fond of Buddha. I've more veneration for that character than for any other – that boldness, that fearlessness, and that tremendous love! He was born for the good of men. He sought truth because people were in misery – how to help them, was his only concern.

And consider his marvellous brain! Believe not because an old manuscript says so, but think for yourself, search truth for yourself, realise it yourself — then if you find it beneficial, give it to people.

And consider his death. He ate food offered to him by an outcast, a *chandal.* He told his disciples not to eat this food: 'but I cannot refuse it; go to the man and tell him he has done me one of the greatest services of my life; he has released me from this body.'

His method of work and organisation was quite striking. The idea that we have today of Church is his creation. He organised the monks and made them into a body. Even the voting by ballot is there, 560 years before Christ. **It was the foundation of Christian religion**; the Catholic Church came from Buddhism.

He was the only man who was even ready to give up his life for animals to stop a sacrifice. He once said to a king, 'If the sacrifice of a lamb helps you to go to heaven, sacrificing a man will help you better. So sacrifice me.' This man set in motion the highest moral ideas any people can have.

To many the path becomes easier if they believe in God. But the life of Buddha shows that even a man who does not believe in God, has no metaphysics, belongs to no sect and goes not to any church, or temple, and is a confessed materialist, even he can attain to the highest.

The Buddha of Light at Nara, in Japan.
53½ feet in height.

Editorspeak

'Make compassion the plinth of religions'

The title of this note has been lifted from a news item published in the Times of India, dated 18 Nov. 09, under Sameer Arshad's name. If cheers this writer no end, because he has been promoting Buddhist ideas—in all the books of the present series—as the saviour from terrorism, creating havoc in the modern world. The authors of this new movement have taken up the essence of this great religion by choosing the word 'compassion' as the guiding force—though they have done very grave injustice by denying it its credit, and, instead, by declaring in their Charter of Compassion, that this principle 'lies at the heart of all religions', not a fact of history; also, fortunately, supported by the spokes-person, Karen Armstrong's works themselves, specially 'Jerusalem', a huge volume examining Abraham's all three religions in the context of this troubled city, and which I've just finished and which has left me really and truly astounded.

But, leaving this discussion for some other occasion, I would move forward by just stating that 'Compassion' is the Brand word—to use modern terminology— of Lord Buddha and his great religion, and no one should try to rob it in broad daylight ... please, please, give the right ones their due, and have the courage to criticise the wrong ones in total humanity's interest.

Well, the Charter of Compassion is a significant achievement of the 21st century, and also an indication that our publicmen and thinkers are proceeding on the right lines. It was unexpected and surprising. I'll, therefore, detail its premises.

I'm a fan of Karen Armstrong ever since I read about her 'A History of God', and am trying to acquire as many of her books as possible, from England, of course, and am overwhelmed by her aptitude, hard work, scholarship, quality of writing—and most of all, proactive vision of the future. I'm pleased to find that she is at the centre of this timely effort. Let me quote the news-item itself:

'Former Roman catholic nun and one of the leading thinkers on the role of religion in the modern world, Karen Armstrong; joined religious leaders from around the globe last week to unveil a Charter of Compassion that calls for return to the ancient principle that **any interpretation of scripture spreading violence or hatred or disdain is illegitimate.**

'The Charter is an attempt to counter highly organized and networked terrorists and extremists. "We must do the same," Armstrong told reporters. The **Charter calls for restoring compassion to the centre of morality and religion** and ensuring that youth are given accurate information about other traditions, religions and cultures "to encourage a positive appreciation of cultural and religious diversity and cultivate an informed empathy with the suffering of all human beings."'

How the Charter was planned and organised is interesting:

'The Charter used a unique web-based decision-making platform to which thousands from over 100 countries added their voices. Thousands of submissions were entered which were then read and commented on by over 150,000 visitors to the website. A Council of Conscience then sorted out the contributions to craft the final Charter document.

'The Charter's 12,499 affirmers include Tibetan spiitual leader Dalai Lama, Jordan's queen Noor, musician Paul Simon, archbishop Desmond Tutu, author and thinker Deepak Chopra and Egypt's Grand Mufti Sheikh Ali Gomaa, among a host of others.'

The Charter boldly puts forth:

'The principle of compassion "lies at the heart of all religious ethical and spirtual traditions, calling us always to treat all others as we wish to be treated outselves." It says, compassion impels people to work to alleviate the suffering of fellow creatures, to dethrone themselves from the centre of the world and put another there, and to honour the inviolable sanctity of every human being, treating everbody without exception, with absolute justice, equity and respect.

"It's also necessary in both public and private life to refrain consistently and emphatically from inflicting pain. To act or speak violently out of spite, chauvinism or self-interest to impoverish, exploit or deny basic rights to anybody, and to incite hatred by denigrating others—even our enemies—is a denial of our common humanity," the Charter says.

'It acknowledges that people have failed to live compassionately and that some have even increased the sum of human misery in the name of religion. "We urgently need to make compassion a clear, luminous and dynamic force in our polarized world. Rooted in a principled determination to transcened selfishness, compassion can break down poltical, dogmatic, ideolgical and religious boudnaries," it says.'

Finally, Karen Armstrong declares:

'The launch of the Charter is the beginning of a voyage and not the end. Now people have their own websites where they can organise and we can make it a movement," Well said and very well initiated. May dear dear dear Karen's Arm prove Strong enough to bring about the much needed change!

It is notable that a few senior Muslims have also joined the movement, and it can be hoped that more will come forward and promote the positive aspects of Islam, curbing this negative one in particular.

Buddhism has been humanity's oldest religion of peace. It spread all over the then known world, and succeeded in pacifying the most violent Mongol cultures of those times.

Fortunately, it is still alive, and has started kicking in the West courtesy chiefly the Dalai Lama. The Japanese Fuji Guruji's movement to establish Peace Pagodas all over the world could be revived and fruitfully utilised for the purpose. The Japanese as a nation can come forward and contribute mightily to it; they will also emerge as great peacemakers, helping to cleanse their image as nasty warmongers.

• • •

The present set of select books on the life, discourses and teachings of Lord Buddha, tries to provide some of the best material on the subject in its as-far-as possible original form. The 'Buddha-Charita' of Asvaghosha, translated most ably by E.B. Cowell, covered the life of the Great Lord till he proclaimed the Wheel of Law in Bodh Gaya, though a fast survey of the spread of his religion is presented in the last few pages. Assuming that this part of his life wouldn't have been of general interest, though he was a great organiser as well as visualiser, who gave the first Church (the Vedics didn't have any such thing) to the world, with an enormous set of rules—and this should also be systematically researched—I've selected the 'Mahaparinibbana Sutta', the seventh chapter of Digha Nikaya—not the 'Mahaparinirvana Sutra' which is in Sanskrit and deals with the subject differently—which provides the most unique and highly moving story of the last eventful days of his life. This Pali work has also been regarded as quite ancient and genuine. Going through it one feels like watching and listening to the Lord himself. The beautiful story of the dancer Amrapali forms part of it.

An addition to the main text is the famous 'Sukhavati Vyuha', or the Land of Bliss, which is a picture of the heaven as visualised by the later day Mahayana Buddhists, and which seems to have been the chief instrument of the spread of Buddhism in the eastern lands of Asia, China, Japan and Korea. The Sukhavati heaven is said to have been planned and created by an earlier Buddha, Amitabha, therefore, our historical Gotama Buddha would certainly have gone out to live there after his decease. It is a rich, cheerful place, fit to be included in the present book. The volume following it is the 'Dhammapada', the Gita of the religion, and most popular among the laity, with the special exercises of Buddhist meditations. This in my view, concludes the first full circle of Buddha scriptures for the modern enthusiast.

Buddham Sharanam . . .

• • •

Contents

Peace be!

Buddha, at Java

1

Buddha at Rajagaha

Thus have I heard:

The Blessed One was once dwelling in Rajagaha, on the hill called the Vulture's Peak. Now at that time Ajatasattu, the son of the queen-consort of Videha origin, the king of Magadha, was desirous of attacking the Vajjians; and he said to himself, 'I will root out these Vajjians, mighty and powerful though they be, I will destroy these Vajjians, I will bring these Vajjians to utter ruin!'

So he spake to the Brahmin Vassakara, the prime minister of Magadha, and said:

'Come now, O Brahmin, do you go to the Blessed One, and bow down in adoration at his feet on my behalf, and enquire in my name whether he is free from illness and suffering, and in the enjoyment of ease and comfort, and vigorous health. Then tell him that Ajatasattu, son of the Vedehi, the king of Magadha, in his eagerness to attack the Vajjians, has resolved, "I will root out these Vajjians, mighty and powerful though they be, I will destroy these Vajjians, I will bring these Vajjians to utter ruin!" And bear carefully in mind whatever the Blessed One may predict, and repeat it to me. For the Buddhas speak nothing untrue!'

Then the Brahmin Vassakara hearkened to the words of the king, saying, 'Be it as you say.' And ordering a number of magnificent carriages to be made ready, he mounted one of them, left Rajagaha with his train, and went to the Vulture's Peak, riding as far as the ground was passable for carriages, and then alighting and proceeding on foot to the place where the Blessed One was. On arriving there he exchanged with the Blessed One the greetings and compliments of friendship and civility, sat down respectfully by his side and then delievered to him the message as the king had commanded.

Now at that time the venerable Ananda was standing behind the Blessed One, and fanning him. And the Blessed One said to him, 'Have you heard, Ananda, that the Vajjians hold full and frequent public assemblies?'

'Lord, so I have heard,' replied he.

'So long, Ananda,' rejoined the Blessed One, 'as the Vajjians hold these full and frequent public assembling; so long may they be expected not to decline, but to prosper.'

And in like manner questioning Ananda, and receiving a similar reply, the Blessed One declared as follows the other conditions which would ensure the welfare of the Vajjian confederacy:

'So long, Ananda, as the Vajjians meet together in concord, and rise in concord, and carry out their undertakings in concord—so long as they enact nothing not already enacted, abrogate nothing that has been already enacted, and act in accordance with the ancient institutions of the Vajjians as established in former days—so long as they honour and esteem and revere and support the Vajjian elders, and hold it as a point of duty to hearken to their words—so long as no women or girls belonging to their clans are detained among them by force or abduction—so long as they honour and esteem and revere and support the Vajjian shrines in town or country, and allow not the proper offerings and rites, as formerly given and performed, to fall into disuse—so long as the rightful protection, defence and support shall be fully provided for the Arahats among them, so that Arahats from a distance may enter the realm, and the Arahats therein may live at ease—so long may the Vajjians be expected not to decline, but to prosper.'

Then the Blessed One addressed Vassakara the Brahmin, and said:

'When I was once staying, O Brahmin, at Vesali at the Sarandada Temple, I taught the Vajjians these conditions of welfare; and so long as those conditions shall continue to exist among the Vajjians, so long as the Vajjians shall be well instructed in those conditions, so long may we expect them not to decline, but to prosper.'

'We may expect, then,' answered the Brahmin, 'the welfare and not the decline of the Vajjians when they are possessed of any one of these conditions of welfare, how much more so when they are possessed of all the seven. So, Gotama, the Vajjians cannot be overcome by the king of Magadha; that is, not in battle, without diplomacy or breaking up their alliance. And now, Gotama, we must go; we are busy, and have much to do.'

'Whatever you think most fitting, O Brahmin,' was the reply. And the Brahmin Vassakara, delighted and pleased with the words of the Blessed One, rose from his seat and went his way.

Conditions of Welfare

Now soon after he had gone, the Blessed One addressed the venerable Ananda, and said: 'Go now, Ananda, and assemble in the Service Hall such of the brethren as live in the neighbourhood of Rajagaha.'

And he did so; and returned to the Blessed One; and informed him, saying:

'The company of the brethren, Lord, is assembled, let the Blessed One do as seemeth to him fit.'

And the Blessed One arose, and went to the Service Hall; and when he was seated, he addressed the brethren, and said:

'I will teach you, O mendicants, seven conditions of the welfare of a community. Listen well and attend, and I will speak.'

'Even so, Lord,' said the brethren, in assent, to the Blessed One; and he spake as follows:

'So long, O mendicants, as the brethren meet together in full and frequent assemblies—so long as they meet together in concord, and rise in concord, and carry out in concord the duties of the order—so long as the brethren shall establish nothing that has not been already prescribed, and abrogate nothing that has been already established and act in accordance with the rules of the order as now laid down—so long as the brethren honour and esteem and revere and support the elders of experience and long standing, the fathers and leaders of the order, and hold it a point of duty to hearken to their words—so long as the brethren fall not under the influence of that craving which, springing up within them, would give rise to renewed existence—so long as the brethren so train their minds that good and holy men shall come to them, and those who have come shall dwell at ease—so long may the brethren be expected not to decline, but to prosper: So long as these seven conditions shall continue to exist among the brethren, so long as they are well-instructed in these conditions, so long may the brethren be expected not to decline, but to prosper.

'Other seven conditions of welfare will I teach you, O brethren. Listen well, and attend, and I will speak.'

And on their expressing their assent, he spake as follows:

'So long as the brethren shall not engage in, or be fond of, or be connected with business—so long as the brethren shall not be in the habit of, or be fond of, or be partakers in idle talk—so long as the brethren shall not be addicted to, or be fond of, or indulge in slothfulness—so long as the brethren shall not frequent, or be fond of, or indulge in society—so long as the brethren shall neither have, nor fall under the influence of sinful desires—so long as the brethren shall not become the friends, companions, or intimates of sinners—so long as the brethren shall not come to a stop on their way to Nirvana because they have attained to any lesser thing—so long may the brethren be expected not to decline, but to prosper.

'So long as these conditions shall continue to exist among the brethren, so long as they are instructed in these conditions, so long may the brethren be expected not to decline, but to prosper.'

'Other seven conditions of welfare will I teach you, O brethren. Listen well, and attend, and I will speak.'

And on their expressing their assent, he spake as follows:

'So long as the brethren shall be full of faith, modest in heart, afraid of sin, full of learning, strong in energy, active in mind, and full of wisdom, so long may the brethren be expected not to decline, but to prosper.

'So long as these conditions shall continue to exist among the brethren, so long as they are instructed in these conditions, so long may the brethren be expected not to decline, but to prosper.'

'Other seven conditions of welfare will I teach you, O brethren. Listen well, and attend, and I will speak.'

And on their expressing their assent, he spake as follows:

'So long as the brethren shall exercise themselves in the sevenfold higher wisdom, that is to say, in mental activity, search after truth, energy, joy, peace, earnest contemplation, and equanimity of mind, so long may the brethren be expected not to decline, but to prosper.

'So long as these conditions shall continue to exist among the brethren, so long as they are instructed in these conditions, so long may the brethren be expected not to decline, but to prosper.'

'Other seven conditions of welfare will I teach you, O brethren. Listen well, and attend, and I will speak.'

And on their expressing their assent, he spake as follows:

'So long as the brethren shall experience themselves in the sevenfold perception due to earnest thought, that is to say, the perception of impermanency, of non-individuality, of corruption, of the danger of sin, of sanctification, of purity of heart, of Nirvana, so long may the brethren be expected not to decline, but to prosper.

'So long as these conditions shall continue to exist among the brethren, so long as they are instructed in these conditions, so long may the brethren be expected not to decline, but to prosper.

'Six conditions of welfare will I teach you, O brethren. Listen well, and attend, and I will speak.'

And on their expressing their assent, he spake as follows:

'So long as the brethren shall persevere in kindness of action, speech, and thought amongst the saints, both in public and in private—so long as they shall divide without partiality, and share in common with the upright and the holy, all such things as they receive in accordance with the just provisions of the order, down even to the mere contents of a begging bowl—so long as the brethren shall live among the saints in the practice, both in public and in private, of those virtues which unbroken, intact, unspotted, unblemished are productive of freedom, and praised by the wise; which are untarnished by the desire by the wise; which are untarnished by the desire of future life; or by the belief in the efficacy of outward acts; and which are conducive to high and holy thoughts—so long as the brethren shall live among the saints, cherishing, both in public and in private, that noble and saving faith which leads to the complete destruction of the sorrow of him who acts according to it—so long may the brethren be expected not to decline, but to prosper.

'So long as these six conditions shall continue to exist among the brethren, so long as they are instructed in these six conditions, so long may the brethren be expected not to decline, but to prosper.'

And whilst the Blessed One stayed there at Rajagaha on Vulture's Peak, he held that comprehensive religious talk with the brethren on the nature of upright conduct, and of earnest contemplation, and of intelligence. 'Great is the fruit, great the advantage of earnest contemplation when set round with upright conduct. Great is the fruit, great the advantages of intellect when set round with earnest contemplation. The mind set round with intelligence is freed from the great evils, that is to say, from sensuality, from individuality, from delusion, and from ignorance.'

Now when the Blessed One had sojourned at Rajagaha as long as he pleased, he addressed the venerable Ananda, and said: 'Come, Ananda, let us go to Ambalatthika.

'So be it, Lord!' said Ananda in assent, and the Blessed One, with a large company of the brethren, proceeded to Ambalatthika.'

There the Blessed One stayed in the king's house and held that comprehensive religious talk with the brethren on the nature of upright conduct, and of earnest contemplation, and of intelligence.

'Great is the fruit, great the advantages of earnest contemplation when set round with upright conduct. Great is the fruit, great the advantages of intellect when set round with earnest contemplation. The mind set round with intelligence is freed from the great evils, that is to say, from sensuality, from individuality, from delusion, and from ignorance.'

With Sariputta at Nalanda

Now when the Blessed One had stayed as long as was convenient at Ambalatthika, he addressed the venerable Ananda, and said, 'Come, Ananda, let us go on to Nalanda.'

'So be it, Lord!' said Ananda, in assent, to the Blessed One.

Then the Blessed One proceeded, with a great company of the brethren, to Nalanda; and there, at Nalanda, the Blessed One stayed in the Pavarika mango grove.

Now the venerable Sariputta came to the place where the Blessed One was, and having saluted him, took his seat respectfully at his side and said: 'Lord! such faith have I in the Blessed One, that methinks there never has been, nor will there be, nor is there now any other, whether Samana of Brahmin, who is greater and wiser than the Blessed One, that is to say, as regards the higher wisdom.'

'Grand and bold are the words of thy mouth, Sariputta, verily, thou hast burst forth into a song of ecstasy! of course then thou hast known all the Blessed Ones who in the long ages of the past have been Arahat Buddhas, comprehending their minds with yours, and aware what their conduct was, what their doctrine, what their wisdom, what their mode of life, and what salvation they attained to?'

'Not so, O Lord!'

'Of course then thou perceived all the Blessed Ones who in the long ages of the future shall be Arahat Buddhas comprehending in the same manner their whole minds with yours?'

'Not so, O Lord!'

'But at least then, O Sariputta, thou knowest means the Arahat now alive, and hast penetrated my mind in the manner I have mentioned!'

'Not even that, O Lord!'

The Blessed one

'You see then, Sariputta, that you know not the hearts of the Arahat Buddhas of the past and of the future. Why therefore are your words so grand and bold? Why do you burst forth into such a song of ecstasy?'

'O Lord! I have not the knowledge of the hearts of the Arahat Buddhas that have been, and are to come, and now are. I only know the lineage of the faith. Just, Lord, as a king might have a border city, strong in its foundations, strong in its ramparts and *toranas*, and with one gate along; and the king might have a watchman there, clever, expert, and wise, to stop all strangers and admit only friends. And he, on going over the approaches all round the city, might not so observe all the joints and crevices in the ramparts of that city as to know where even a cat could get out. That might well be. Yet all living things of larger size that entered or left the city, would have to do so by that gate. Thus only is it, Lord, that I know the lineage of the faith. I know that the Arahat Buddhas of the past, putting away all lust, ill-will, sloth, pride, and doubt; knowing all those mental faults which make men weak; training their minds in the four kinds of mental activity; thoroughly exercising themselves in the sevenfold higher wisdom, received the full fruition of Enlightenment. And I know that the Arahat Buddhas of the times to come will do the same. And I know that the Blessed One, the Arahat Buddha of to-day, has done so now.'

There in the Pavarika mango grove the Blessed One held that comprehensive religious talk with the brethren on the nature of upright conduct, and of earnest contemplation, and of intelligence: 'Great is the fruit, great the advantages of earnest contemplation when set round with upright conduct. Great is the fruit, great the advantage of intellect when set round with earnest contemplation. The mind set round with intelligence is freed from the great evils, that is to say, from sensuality, from individuality, from delusion, and from ignorance.'

At Pataligama

Now when the Blessed One had stayed as long as was convenient at Nalarda, he addressed the venerable Ananda, and said: 'Come, Ananda, let us go on to Pataligama.'

'So be it, Lord!' said Ananda, in assent, to the Blessed One.

Then the Blessed One proceeded, with a great company of the brthren, to Pataligama.

Now the disciples at Pataligama heard of his arrival there, and they went to the place where he was, took their seats respectfully beside him, and invited him to their village rest house. And the Blessed One signified, by silence, his consent.

Then the Pataligama disciples seeing that he had accepted the invitation, rose from their seats, and went away to the rest house, bowing to the Blessed One and keeping him on their right as they past him. On arriving there they made the rest house fit in every way for occupation, placed seats in it, set up a water-pot, and fixed an oil lamp. Then they returned to the Blessed One, and bowing, stood beside him, and said: 'All things are ready, Lord! It is time for you to do what you deem most fit.'

And the Blessed One robed himself, took his bowl and other things, went with the brethren to the rest house, washed his feet, entered the hall, and took his seat against the centre pillar, with his face towards the east. And the brethren also, after washing their feet, entered the hall, and took their seats round the Blessed One, against the western wall, and facing the east. And the Pataligama disciples too, after washing their feet, entered the hall, and took their seats opposite the Blessed One, against the eastern wall, and facing towards the west.

Then the Blessed One addressed the Pataligama disciples, and said:

'Fivefold, O householders, is the loss of the wrongdoer through his want of rectitude. In the first place, the wrongdoer, devoid of rectitude, falls into great poverty through sloth; in the next place, his evil repute gets noised abroad; thirdly, whatever society he enters—whether of Brahmins, nobles, heads of houses, or Samanas—he enters shyly and confused; fourthly, he is full of anxiety when he dies; and lastly, on the dissolution of the body, after death, he is reborn into some unhappy state of suffering or woe. This, O housholders, is the fivefold loss of the evildoer!'

'Fivefold, O householders, is the gain of the welldoer through his practice of rectitude. In the first place, the welldoer, strong in rectitude, acquires great wealth through his industry; in the next place, good reports of him are spread abroad; thirdly, whatever society he enters—whether of nobles, Brahmins, heads of houses, or members of the order—he enters confident and self-possessed; fourthly, he dies without anxiety; and lastly, on the dissolution of the body, after death, he is reborn into some happy state in heaven. This, O householders, is the fivefold gain of the welldoor.'

When the Blessed One had thus taught the disciples, and incited them, and roused them, and gladdened them, far into the right with religious discourse, he dismissed them, saying, 'The night is far spent, O householders. It is time for you to do what you deem most fit.'

'Even so, Lord!' answered the disciples of Pataligama, and they rose from their seats, and bowing to the Blessed One, and keeping him on their right hand as they passed him, they departed thence.

And the Blessed One, not long after the disciples of Pataligama had departed thence, entered into his private chamber.

At that time Sunidha and Vassakara, the chief ministers of Magadha, were building a fortress at Pataligama to repel the Vajjians, and there were a number of fairies who haunted in thousands the plots of ground there. Now, wherever ground is so occupied by powerful fairies, they bend the hearts of the most powerful kings and ministers to build dwelling-places there, and fairies of middling and inferior power bend in a similar way the hearts of middling or inferior kings and ministers.

And the Blessed One, with his great and clear vision, surpassing that of ordinary men, saw thousands of those fairies haunting Pataligama. And he rose up very early in the morning, and said to Ananda: 'Who is it then, Ananda, who is building a fortress at Pataligama?

'Sunidha and Vassakara, Lord, the chief ministers of Magadha, are building a fortress there to keep back the Vajjians.'

'They act, Ananda, as if they had consulted with the Tavatimsa angels.' And telling him of what he had seen, and of the influence such fairies had, he added: 'And among famous places of residence and haunts of busy men, this will become the chief, the city of Pataliputta, a centre for the interchange of all kinds of wares. But there dangers will hang over Pataliputta, that of fire, that of water, and that of dissension.'

Now Sunidha and Vassakara, the chief ministers of Magadha, proceeded to the place where the Blessed One was. And when they had come there they exchanged with the Blessed One the greetings and compliments of friendship and civility, and stood there respectfully on one side. And, so standing, Sunidha and Vassakara, the chief ministers of Magadha, spake thus to the Blessed One:

'May the venerable Gotama do us the honour of taking his meal, together with the company of the brethren, at our house today.' And the Blessed One signified, by silence, his consent.

Then when Sunidha and Vassakara, the chief ministers of Magadha, perceived that he had given his consent, they returned to the place where they dwelt. And on arriving there, they prepared sweet dishes of boiled rice, and cakes; and informed the Blessed One, saying:

'The hour of food has come, O Gotama, and all is ready.'

And the Blessed One robed himself early, took his bowl with him and repaired with the brethren to the dwelling-place of Sunidha and Vassakara, and sat down on the seat prepared for him. And with their own hands they set the sweet rice and the cakes before the brethren with the Buddha at their head, and waited on them till they had enough. And when the Blessed One had finished eating his meal, the ministers brought a low seat, and sat down respectfully at his side.

And when they were thus seated, the Blessed One gave thanks in these verses:

'Wheresoe'er the prudent man shall take up his abode

Let him support there good and upright men of self-control.

Let him give gifts to all such deities as may be there.

Revered, they will revere him; honoured, they honour him again;

Are gracious to him as a mother to her own, her only son.

And the man who has the grace of the gods, good fortune he beholds.'

And when he had thanked the ministers in these verses, he rose from his seat and departed thence. And they followed him as he went, saying, 'The gate the Samana Gotama goes out by to-day shall be called Gotama's Gate, and the ferry at which he crosses the river shall be called Gotama's Ferry.' And the gate he went out at was called Gotama's Gate.

Swims across the Ganges

But the Blessed One went on to the river. And at that time the river Ganges was brimful and overflowing; and wishing to cross to the opposite bank, some began to seek for boats, some for rafts of wood, while some made rafts of basketwork. Then the Blessed One as instantaneously as a strong man would stretch forth his arm, or draw it back again when he had stretched it forth, vanished from this side of the river, and stood on the further bank with the company of the brethren.

And the Blessed One beheld the people looking for boats and rafts, and as he beheld them he broke forth at that time into this song:

'They who cross the ocean drear
Making a solid path across the pools—
Whilst the vain world ties its basket rafts—
These are the wise, these are the saved indeed!'

2

Eats at Ambapali's

Now the Blessed One addressed the venerable Ananda, and said: 'Come, Ananda, let us go on to Kotigama.'

'So be it, Lord!' said Ananda, in assent, to the Blessed One.

The Blessed One proceeded with a great company of the brethren to Kotigama; and there he stayed in the village itself.

And at that place the Blessed One addressed the brethren, and said: 'It is through not understanding and grasping four Noble Truths, O brethren, that we have had to run so long, to wander so long in this weary path of transmigration, both you and I!'

'And what are these four?'

'The noble truth about sorrow; the noble truth about the cause of sorrow; the noble truth about the cessation of sorrow; and the noble truth about the path that leads to that cessation. But when these noble truths are grasped and known, the craving for existence is rooted out, that which leads to renewed existence is destroyed, and then there is no more birth!'

Thus spake the Blessed One; and when the Happy One had thus spoken, then again the Teacher said:

'By not seeing the four Noble Truths as they really are,

Dancer, Java

Long is the path that is traversed through many a birth;
When these are grasped, the cause of birth is then removed,
The root of sorrow rooted out, and there is no more birth.'

There too, while staying at Kotigama, the Blessed One held that comprehensive religious discourse with the brethren on the nature of upright conduct, and of earnest contemplation, and of intelligence. 'Great is the fruit, great the advantage of earnest contemplation when set round with upright conduct. Great is the fruit, great the advantage of intellect when set round with earnest contemplation. The mind set round with intelligence is freed from the great evils,— that is to say, from sensuality, from individuality, from delusion, and from ignorance.'

Now when the Blessed One had remained as long as was convient at Kotigama, he addressed the venerable Ananda, and said: 'Come, Ananda, let us go on to the villages of Nadika.'

'So be it, Lord!' said Ananda, in assent, to the Blessed One.

And the Blessed one proceeded to the villages of Nadika with a great company of the brethren; and there, at Nadika, the Blessed One stayed at the Brick Hall.

And the venerable Ananda went to the Blessed One and paid him reverence and took his seat beside him. And when he was seated, he addressed the Blessed One, and said: 'The brother named Salha has died at Nadika, Lord. Where has he been reborn, and what is his destiny? The sister named Nanda has died, Lord, at Nadika. Where is she reborn, and what is her destiny?' And in the same terms he enquired concerning the devout Sudatta, and the devout lady Sujata, the devout Kakudha, and Kalinga, and Nikata, and Katissabha, and Tuttha, and Santuttha, and Bhadda, and Subhadda.

'The brother named Salha, Ananda, by the destruction of the great evils has by himself, and in this world, known and realised and attained to Arahatship, and to emancipation of heart and to emancipation of mind. The sister named Nanda, Ananda, has, by the complete destruction of the five bonds that bind people to this world, become an inheritor of the highest heavens, there to pass entirely away, thence never to return. The devout Sudatta, Ananda, by the complete destruction of the three bonds, and by the reduction to a minimum of lust, hatred, and delusion, has become a Sakadagamin, who on his first return to this world will make an end of sorrow. The devout woman Sujata, Ananda, by the complete destruction of the three bonds, has become converted, is no longer liable to be reborn in a state of suffering, and is assured of final salvation. The devout Kakudha, Ananda, by the complete destruction of the five bonds that bind people to these lower worlds of lust, has become an inheritor of the highest heavens, there to pass entirely away, thence never to return. So also is the case with Kalinga, Nikata, Katissabha, Tuttha, Santuttha, Bhadda and Subhadda, and with more than fifty devout men of Nadika. More than ninety devout men of Nadika, who have died, Ananda, have by the complete destruction of the three bonds, and by the reduction of lust, hatred, and delusion, become Sakadagamins, who on their first return to this world will make an end of sorrow. More than five hundred devout men of Nadika who have died, Ananda, have by the complete destruction of the three bonds become converted, are no longer liable to be reborn in a state of suffering, and are assured of final salvation.

'Now there is nothing strange in this, Ananda, that a human being should die, but that as each one does so you should come to the Buddha, and enquire about them in this manner, that is wearisome to the Buddha. I will, therefore, teach you a way of truth, called the Mirror of Truth, which if an elect disciple possess he may himself predict of himself, "Hell is destroyed for me, and rebirth as an animal, or a ghost, or in any place of woe. I am converted, I am no longer liable to be reborn in a state of suffering, and am assured of final salvation."

'What then, Ananda, is this mirror of truth? It is the consciousness that the elect disciple is in this world possessed of faith in the Buddha—believing the Blessed One to be the Holy One, the Fully-enlightened One, Wise, Upright, Happy, World-knowing, Supreme, the Bridler of men's wayward hearts, the Teacher of gods and men, the Blessed Buddha. And that he, the disciple, is possessed of faith in the Truth—believing the truth to have been proclaimed by the Blessed One, of advantages in this world, passing not away, welcoming all, leading to salvation, and to be attained to by the wise, each one for himself. And that he 'the disciple' is possessed of faith in the Order—believing the multitude of the disciples of the Blessed One who are walking in the four stages of the noble eightfold path, the righteous, the upright, the just, the law-abiding—believing this church of the Buddha to be worthy of honour, of hospitality, of gifts, and of reverence; to be the supreme sowing ground of merit for the world; to be possessed of the virtues beloved by the good virtues unbroken, intact, unspotted, unblemished, virtues which make men truly free, virtues which are praised by the wise, the untarnished by the desire of future life or by the belief in the efficacy of outward acts, and are conducive to high and holy thought.'

'This, Ananda, is the way, the mirror of truth, which if an elect disciple possess he may himself predict of himself: "Hell is destroyed for me; and rebirth as an animal, or a ghost, or in any place of woe. I am converted; I am no longer liable to be reborn in a state of suffering, and am assured of final salvation."'

There, too, at the Brick Hall at Nadika the Blessed One addressed to the brethren that comprehensive religious discourse on the nature of upright conduct, and of earnest contemplation, and of intelligence.

'Great is the fruit, great the advantages of earnest contemplation when set round with upright conduct. Great is the fruit, great the advantages of intellect when set round with earnest contemplation. The mind set round with intelligence is freed from the great evils, that is to say, from sensuality, from individuality, from delusion, and from ignorance.'

Visit to Vesali

Now when the Blessed One had remained as long as he wished at Nadika, he addressed Ananda, and said: 'Come, Ananda, let us go on to Vesali.'

'So be it, Lord!' said Ananda, in assent, to the Blessed One.

Then the Blessed One proceeded, with a great company of the brethren, to Vesali; and there at Vesali the Blessed One stayed at Ambapali's grove.

Now there the Blessed one addressed the brethren, and said: 'Let a brother, O mendicants, be mindful and thoughtful; this is our instruction to you.'

'And how does a brother become mindful?'

'Herein, O mendicants, let a brother, as he dwells in the body, so regard the body that he, being strenuous, thoughtful, and mindful, may, whilst in the world, overcome the grief which arises from bodily craving—while subject to sensations, let him continue so to regard the sensations, let him continue so to regard the sensations that he, being strenuous, thoughtful, and mindful, may, whilst in the world overcome the grief arising from the craving which follows our sensation—and so also as he thinks or reasons or feels, let him overcome the grief which arises from the craving due to ideas, or reasoning, or feeling.'

'And how does a brother become thoughtful?'

'He acts, O mendicants, in full presence of mind whatever he may do, in going out and coming in, in looking and watching, in bending in his arm or stretching it forth, in wearing his robes or carrying his bowl, in eating and drinking, in consuming or tasting, in walking or standing or sitting, in sleeping or walking, in talking and in being silent.

'Thus let a brother, O medicants, be mindful and thoughtful; this is our instruction to you.'

Ambapali invites to a meal

Now the courtesan Ambapali heard that the Blessed One had arrived at Vesali, and was staying at her mango grove. And ordering a number of magnificent vehicles to be made ready, she mounted one of them, and proceeded with her train towards her garden. She went in the carriage as far as the ground was passable for carriages; there she alighted; and she proceeded on foot to the place where the Blessed One was, and took her seat respectfully on one side. And when she was thus seated the Blessed One instructed, aroused, incited, and gladdened her with religious discourse.

Then she—instructed, aroused, incited, and gladdened with his words—addressed the Blessed One, and said:

'May the Blessed One do me the honour or taking his meal, together with the brethren, at my house tomorrow.'

And the Blessed One gave, by silence, his consent. Then when Ambapali the courtesan saw that the Blessed One had consented, she rose from her seat and bowed down before him, and keeping him on her right hand as she past him, she departed thence.

Now the Lichchhavis of Vesali heard that the Blessed One had arrived at Vesali, and was staying at Ambapali's grove. And ordering a number of magnificent carriages to be made ready, they mounted one of them and proceeded with their train to Vesali. Some of them were dark, dark in colour, and wearing dark clothes and ornaments; some of them were fair, fair in colour, and wearing light colour and ornaments; some of them were red, ruddy in colour, and wearing red clothes and ornaments: some of them were

Awaiting

white, pale in colour, and wearing white clothes and ornaments.

And Ambapali drove up against the young Lichchhavis, axle to axle, wheel to wheel, and yoke to yoke, and the Lichchhavis said to Ambapali the courtesan, 'How is it Ambapali, that thou drivest up against us thus?'

'My Lords, I have just invited the Blessed One and his brethren for their morrow's meal,' said she.

'Ambapali! give up this meal to us for a hundred thousand,' said they.

'My Lords, were you to offer all Vesali with its subject territory, I would not give up so honourable a feast!'

Then the Lichchhavis cast up their hands, exclaiming, 'We are outdone by this mango girl! we are outreached by this mango girl!' and they went on to Ambapali's grove.

When the Blessed One saw the Lichchhavis approaching in the distance, he addressed the brethren, and said:

'O brethren, let those of the brethren who have never seen the Tavatimsa gods, gaze upon this company of the Lichchhavis, behold this company of the Lichchhavis, compare this company of the Lichchhavis—even as a company of Tavatimsa gods.'

And when they had ridden as far as the ground was passable for carriages, the Lichchhavis alighted there, and then went on foot to the place where the Blessed One was, and took their seats respectfully by his side. And when they were thus seated, the Blessed One instructed and roused and incited and gladdened them with religious discourse.

Then they instructed and roused and incited and gladdened with his words, addressed the Blessed One, and said, 'May the Blessed One do us the honour of taking his meal, together with the brethren, at our house to-morrow.'

'O Lichchhavis, I have promised to dine to-morrow with Ambapali the courtesan,' was the reply.

Then the Lichchhavis cast up their hands, exclaiming, 'We are outdone by this mango girl! we are outreached by this mango girl!' And expressing their thanks and approval of the words of the Blessed One, they rose from their seats and bowed down before the Blessed One, and keeping him on their right hand as they past him, they departed thence.

And at the end of the night Ambapali the courtesan made ready in her mansion sweet rice and cakes, and announced the time to the Blessed One, saying, 'The hour, Lord, has come, and the meal is ready!'

And the Blessed One robed himself early in the morning, and took his bowl, and went with the brethren to the place where Ambapali's dwelling-house was; and when he had come there he seated himself on the seat prepared for him. And Ambapali the courtesan set the sweet rice and cakes before the order, with the Buddha at their head, and waited upon them till they refused any more.

And when the Blessed One had quite finished his meal, the courtesan had a low stool brought, and sat down at his side, and addressed the Blessed One, and said: 'Lord, I present this mansion to the order of mendicants, of which the Buddha is the chief.' And the Blessed One accepted the gift; and after instructing, and rousing, and inciting, and gladdening her with religious discourse, he rose from his seat and departed thence.

While at Ambapali's mango grove the Blessed One held that comprehensive religious discourse with the disciples on the nature of upright conduct, and of earnest contemplation, and of intelligence:

'Great is the fruit, great the advantages of earnest contemplation when set round with upright conduct. Great is the fruit, great the advantages of intellect when set round with earnest contemplation. The mind set round with intelligence is freed from the great evils, that is to say, from sensuality, from individuality, from delusion, and from ignorance.'

Now when the Blessed One had remained as long as he wished at Ambapali's grove, he addressed Ananda, and said: 'Come, Ananda, let us go on to Beluva.'

'So be it, Lord,' said Ananda, in assent, to the Blessed One.

Then the Blessed One proceeded, with a great company of the brethren, to Beluva, and there the Blessed One stayed in the village itself.

Now the Blessed One there addressed the brethren, and said: 'O mendicants, do you take up your abode round Vesali, each according to the place where his friends, intimates, and close companions may live, for the rainy season of Vassa. I shall enter upon the rainy season here at Beluva.'

'So be it, Lord!' said those brethren, in assent, to the Blessed One. And they entered upon the rainy season round about Vesali, each according to the place where his friends or intimates or close companious lived; whilst the Blessed One stayed even there at Beluva.

Buddha is sick

Now when the Blessed One had thus entered upon the rainy season, there fell upon him a dire sickness, and sharp pains came upon him, even unto death. But the Blessed One, mindful and self-possessed, bore them without complaint.

Then this thought occurred to the Blessed One, 'It would not be right for me to pass away from existence without addressing the disciples, without taking leave of the order. Let me now, by a strong effort of the will, bend this sickness down again, and keep my hold on life till the allotted time be come.'

And the Blessed One, by a strong effort of the will, bent that sickness down again, and kept his hold on life till the time he fixed upon should come. And the sickness abated upon him.

Now very soon after the Blessed One began to recover; when he had quite got rid of the sickness, he went out from the monastery, and sat down behind the monastery on a seat spread out there. And the venerable Ananda went to the place where the Blessed One was, and saluted him, and took a seat respectfully on one side, and addressed the Blessed One, and said: 'I have beheld, Lord, how the Blessed One was in health, and I have beheld how the Blessed One had to suffer. And though at the sight of the sickness of the Blessed One my body became weak as a creeper, and the horizon became dim to me, and my faculties were no longer clear, yet not with-standing I took some little comfort from the thought that the Blessed One would not pass away from existence until at least he had left instructions as touching the order,'

'What, then, Ananda? Does the order expect that of me? I have preached the truth without making any distinction between exoteric and esoteric doctrine; for in respect of the truths, Ananda, the Tathagata has no such thing as the closed fist of a teacher, who keeps some things back. Surely, Ananda, should there be any one who harbours the thought, "It is I who will lead the brotherhood," or, "The order is dependent upon me," it is he who should lay down instructions in any matter concerning the order. Now the Tathagata, Ananda,thinks not that it is he who should lead the brotherhood, or that the order is dependent upon him. Why then should he leave instructions in any matter concerning the order? I too, O Ananda, am now grown old, and full of years, my journey is drawing to its close, I have reached my sum of days, I am turning eighty years of age; and just as a worn-out cart, Ananda, can only with much additional care be made to move along, so, methinks, the body of the Tathagata can only be kept going with much additional care. It is only, Ananda, when the Tathagata, ceasing to attend to any outward thing, or to experience any sensation, becomes plunged in that devout meditation of heart which is concerned with no material object—it is only then that the body of the Tathagata is at ease.

'Therefore, O Ananda, **be ye lamps unto youselves. Be ye a refuge. Hold fast to the truth as a lamp. Hold fast as a refuge to the truth. Look not for refuge to any one besides yourselves.** And how, Ananda, is a brother to be lamp unto himself, a refuge to himself, betaking himself to no external refuge, holding fast to the truth as a lamp, holding fast as a refuge to the truth, looking not for refuge to any one besides himself?

'Herein, O Ananda, let a brother, as he dwells in the body, so regard the body that he, being strenuous, thoughtful, and mindful, may, whilst in the world, overcome the grief which arises from bodily craving—while subject to sensations let him continue so to regard the sensations that he, being strenuous, thoughtful and mindful, may, whilst in the world, overcome the grief which arises from the sensations—and so, also, as he thinks, or reasons, or feels, let him overcome the grief which arises from the craving due to ideas, or to reasoning or to feeling.

'And whosoever, Ananda, either now or after I am dead, shall be a lamp unto themselves, and a refuge unto themselves, shall betake themselves to no external refuge, but holding fast to the truth as their lamp, and holding fast as their refuge to the truth, shall look not for refuge to any one besides themselves—it is they, Ananda, among my bhikkhus, who shall reach the very topmost height!—but they must be anxious to learn.'

3

Sickness

Now the Blessed One robed himself early in the morning, and taking his bowl in the robe, went into Vesali for alms, and when he returned, he sat down on the seat prepared for him, and after he had finished eating the rice, he addressed the venerable Ananda, and said: 'Take up the mat, Ananda; I will go to spend the day at the Chapala Chetiya.'

'So be it, Lord!' said the venerable Ananda, in assent, to the Blessed One. And taking up the mat he followed step for step behind the Blessed One.

So the Blessed One proceeded to the Chapala Chetiya, and when he had come there he sat down on the mat spread out for him, and the venerable Ananda took his seat respectfully beside him. Then the Blessed One addressed the venerable Ananda and said: 'How delightful a spot, Ananda, is Vesali, and the Udena Chetiya, and the Gotamaka Chetiya, and the Sattambaka Chetiya, and Bahuputta Chetiya, and the Sarandada Chetiya, and the Chapala Chetiya.

'Ananda! whosoever has thought out, developed, practised, accumulated, and ascended to the very heights of the four paths to Iddhi, and so mastered them as to be able to use them as a means of mental advancement, and as a basis for edification, he, should he desire it, could remain in the same birth for a kalpa, or for that portion of the kalpa which had yet to run. Now the Tathagata has thought them in all respects as just more fully described, and he could therefore, should he desire it, live on yet for a kalpa, or for that portion of the kalpa which has yet to run.'

But even though a suggestion so evident and a hint so clear were thus given by the Blessed One, the venerable Ananda was incapable of comprehending them; and he besought not the Blessed One, saying, 'Vouchsafe, Lord, to remain during the kalpa! Live on through the kalpa, O Blessed One! for the good and the happiness of the great multitudes, out of pity for the world, for the good and the gain and the weal of gods and men!' So far was his heart possessed by Mara, the Evil One.

A second and a third time did the Blessed One say the same thing, and a second and a third time was Ananda's heart thus hardened.

Now the Blessed One addressed the venerable Ananda, and said: 'You may leave me, Ananda, a while, and do whatever seemeth to thee fit.'

'So be it, Lord!' said the venerable Ananda, in assent, to the Blessed, and rising from his seat he saluted the Blessed One, and passing him on the right, sat down at the foot of a certain tree not far off thence.

'Pass away now,' says Mara

Now not long after the venerable Ananda had been gone, Mara, the Evil One, approached the Blessed One, and stood beside him. And so standing there, he addressed the Blessed One in these words:

'Pass away now, Lord, from existence; let the Blessed One now die. Now is the time for the Blessed One to pass away—even according to the word which the Blessed One spoke when he said: "I shall not die, O Evil One! until the brethren and sisters of the order, until the lay disciples of either sex shall have become true hearers, wise and well-

Stuck!

trained, ready and learned, versed in the scriptures, fulfiling all the greater and the lesser duties, correct in life, walking according to the precepts—until they, having thus themselves learned the doctrine, shall be able to tell others of it, preach it, make it known, establish it, open it, minutely explain it and make it clear—until they, when others start vain doctrines, shall be able by the truth to vanquish and refute it, and so to spread the wonder-working truth abroad!"

'And now, Lord, the brethren and sisters of the order and the lay disciples of either sex have become all this, are able to do. Pass away now therefore, Lord, from existence; let the Blessed One now die! The time has come for the Blessed One to pass away—even according to the word which he spake when he said, "I shall not die, O Evil One! until this pure religion of mine shall have become successful, prosperous, widespread, and popular in all its full extent—until, in a word, it shall have been well proclaimed to men." And now, Lord, this pure religion of thine has become all this. Pass away now therefore, Lord, from existence; let the Blessed One now die! The time has come for the Blessed One to pass away!'

And when he had thus spoken, the Blessed One addressed Mara, the Evil One, and said: 'O Evil One! make thyself happy, the final extinction of the Tathagata shall take place before long. At the end of three months from this time the Tathagata will die!'

Thus the Blessed One, while at the Chapala Chetiya, deliberately and consciouly rejected the rest of his allotted sum of life. And on his so rejecting it there arose a mighty earthquake, awful and terrible, and the thunders of heaven burst forth. And when the Blessed One beheld this, he broke out at that time into this hymn of exultation:

'His sum of life the sage renounced,
The cause of life immeasurable or small;
With inward joy and calm, he broke,
Like coat of mail, his life's own cause!'

Now the following thought occurred to the venerable Ananda: 'Wonderful indeed and marvellous is it that this mighty earthquake should arise, awful and terrible, and that the thunders of heaven should burst forth! What may be the proximate, what the remote cause of the appearance of this earthquake?'

Then the venerable Ananda went up to the place where the Blessed One was, and did obeisance to the Blessed One, and seated himself respectfully at one side, and said: 'Wonderful indeed and marvellous is it that this mighty earthquake should arise, awful and terrible, and that the thunders of heaven should burst forth! What may be the proximate, what the remote cause of the appearance of this earthquake?'

'Eight are the proximate, eight the remote causes, Ananda, for the appearance of a mighty earthquake. What are the eight? This great earth, Ananda, is established on water, the water on wind, and the wind rests upon space. And at such a time, Ananda, as the mighty winds blow, the waters are shaken by the mighty winds as they blow, and by the moving water the earth is shaken. These are the first causes, proximate and remote, of the appearance of a mighty earthquake.

'Again, Ananda, a Samana or a Brahmin of great intellectual power, and who has the feelings of his heart well under his control; or a god or fairy of great might and power—when such a one by intense meditation of the finite idea of earth or the infinite idea of water has succeeded in realising the comparative value of things, he can make this earth move and tremble and be shaken violently. These are the second causes, proximate or remote, of the appearance of a mighty earthquake.

'Again, Ananda, when a Bodhisattva consciously and deliberately leaves his temporary form in the heaven of delight and descends into his mother's womb, then is this earth made to quake and tremble and is shaken violently.

These are the third causes, proximate or remote, of the appearance of a mighty earthquake.

'Again, Ananda, when a Bodhisattva deliberately and consciously quits his mother's womb, then the earth quakes and trembles and is shaken violently. This is the fourth cause, proximate and remote, of the appearance of a mighty earthquake.

'Again, Ananda, when a Tathagata arrives at the supreme and perfect enlightenment, then this earth quakes and trembles and is shaken violently. This is the fifth cause, proximate and remote, of the appearance of a mighty earthquake.

'Again, Ananda, when a Tathagata founds the sublime kingdom of righteousness, then this earth quakes and trembles and is shaken violently. This is the sixth cause, proximate and remote, of the appearance of a mighty earthquake.

'Again, Ananda, when a Tathagata consciously and deliberately rejects the remainder of his life, then this earth quakes and trembles and is shaken violently. This is the seventh cause, proximate and remote, of the appearance of a mighty earthquake.

'Again, Ananda, when a Tathagata passes entirely away with that utter passing away in which nothing whatever is left behind, then this earth quakes and trembles and is shaken violently. This is the eighth cause, proximate and remote, of the appearance of a mighty earthquake.'

The eight kinds

'Now of eight kinds, Ananda, are these assemblies. Which are the eight? Assemblies of nobles, Brahmins, householders, and Samanas, and the angel hosts of the Guardian Angels, the Great Thirty-Three, Mara, and Brahma.

'Now I call to mind, Ananda, how when I used to enter into an assembly of many hundred nobles, before I had seated myself there or talked to them or started a conversation with them, I used to become in colour like unto their colour, and in voice like unto their voice. Then with religious discourse I used to instruct, incite and quicken them, and fill them with gladness. But they knew me not when I spoke, and would say, "Who may this be who thus speaks? a man or a god?" Then having instructed, incited, quickened, and gladdened them with religious discourse, I would vanish away. But they knew me not even when I vanished away; and would say, "Who may this be who has thus vanished away? a man or a god?"'

And in the same words the Blessed One spake of how he had been used to enter into assemblies of each of the other of the eight kinds, and of how he had not been made known to them either in speaking or in vanishing away. 'Now these, Ananda, are the eight assemblies.'

'Now these, Ananda, are the eight positions of mastery over the delusion arising from the apparent permanence of external things. What are the eight?

'When a man having subjectively the idea of form sees externally forms which are finite, and pleasant or unpleasant to the sight, and having mastered them, is conscious that he knows and sees—this is the first position of mastery.

'When a man having subjectively the idea of form sees externally forms which are boundless, and pleasant or unpleasant to the sight, and having mastered them, is conscious that he knows and sees—this is the second position of mastery.

'When a man without the subjective idea of form sees externally forms which are finite, and pleasant or unpleasant to the sight, and having mastered them, is conscious that he knows and sees—this is the third position of mastery.

'When a man without the subjective idea of form sees externally forms which are boundless, and pleasant or unpleasant to the sight, and having mastered them, is conscious that he knows and sees—this is the fourth position of mastery.

'When a man without the subjective idea of form sees externally forms that are blue in colour, blue in appearance, and reflecting blue,—just, for instance, as the Umma flower is blue in colour, blue in appearance, and reflecting blue; or, again, as that fine muslin of Benares which, on whichever side you look at it, is blue in colour, blue in appearance, and reflecting blue,—when a man without the subjective idea of form sees externally forms which, just in that way, are blue, blue in colour, blue in appearance, and reflecting blue, and having mastered them, is conscious that he knows and sees—that is the fifth position of mastery.'

(The sixth, seventh, and eight positions of mastery are explained in words identical with those used to explain the fifth; save that yellow, red, and white are respectively substituted throughout for blue; and the Kanikara flower, the Bandhu-jivaka flower, and the morning star are respectively substituted for the Umma flower, as the first of the two objects given as examples.)

'Now these stages of deliverance, Ananda, from the hindrance to thought arising from the sensations and ideas due to external forms, are eight in number. Which are the eight?

'A man possessed with the idea of form sees forms—this is the first stage of deliverance.

'Without the subjective idea of form, he sees forms externally—this is the second stage of deliverance.

'With the thought "it is well," he becomes intent upon what he sees—this is the third stage of deliverance.

'By passing quite beyond all idea of form, by putting an end to all idea of resistance, by paying no attention to the idea of distinction, he, thinking "it is all infinite space,"

Men and angels adoring a stupa. Bharhut, second century B.C.

reaches mentally and remains in the state of mind in which the idea of the infinity of space is the only idea that is present—this is the fourth stage of deliverance.

'By passing quite beyond all idea of space being the infinite basis, he, thinking "it is all infinite reason," reaches mentally and remains in the state of mind to which the infinity of reason is alone present—this is the fifth stage of deliverance.

'By passing quite beyond the mere consciousness of the infinity of reason, he thinking "nothing at all exists," reaches mentally and remains in the state of mind to which nothing at all is specially present—this is the sixth stage of deliverance.

'By passing quite beyond all idea of nothingness he reaches mentally and remains in the state of mind to which neither ideas nor the absence of ideas are specially present—this is the seventh stage of deliverance.

'By passing quite beyond the state of "neither ideas nor the absence of ideas" he reaches mentally and remains in the state of mind in which both sensations and ideas have ceased to be—this is the eighth stage of deliverance.

'Now these, Ananda, are the eight stages of deliverance.'

'I'll die after three months'

'On one occasion, Ananda, I was resting under the shepherd's Nigrodha tree on the bank on the river Neranjara immediately after having reached the great enlightenment. Then Mara, the Evil One, came, Ananda, to the place, where I was, and standing beside me he addressed me in the words: "Pass away now, Lord, from existence! Let the Blessed One now die! Now is the time for the Blessed One to pass away!"

'And when he had thus spoken, Ananda, I addressed Mara, the Evil One, and said: "I shall not die, O Evil One! until not only the brethren and sisters of the order, but also the lay disciples of either sex shall have become true hearers, wise and well-trained, ready and learned, versed in the scriptures, fulfilling all the greater and the lesser duties, correct in life, walking according to the precepts—until they, having thus themselves learned the doctrine, shall be able to tell others of it, preach it, make it known, establish it, open it, minutely explain it and make it clear—until they, when others start vain doctrines, shall be able by the truth to vanquish and refute it, and so to spread the wonder-working truth abroad!

"'I shall not die until this pure religion of mine shall have become successful, prosperous, widespread, and popular in all its full extent—until, in a word, it shall have been well proclaimed among men!"

'And now again to-day, Ananda, at the Chapala Chetiya, Mara, the Evil One, came to the place where I was, and standing beside me, addressed me in the same words.

'And when he had thus spoken, Ananda, I answered him and said: "Make thyself happy, the final extinction of the Tathagata shall take place before long. At the end of three months from this time the Tathagata will die!'

'Thus, Ananda, the Tathagata has now to-day at the Chapala Chetiya consciously and deliberately rejected the rest of his allotted term of life.'

And when he had thus spoken the venerable Ananda addressed the Blessed One, and said: 'Vouchsafe, Lord, to remain during the kalpa! live on through the kalpa, O Blessed One! for the good and the happiness of the great multitudes, out of pity for the world, for the good and the gain and the weal of gods and men!'

'Enough now, Ananda, beseech not the Tathagata!' was the reply. 'The time for making such request is past.'

And again the second time, the venerable Ananda besought the Blessed One in the same words. And he received from the Blessed One the same reply.

And again, the third time, the venerable Ananda besought the Blessed One in the same words.

'Hast thou faith, Ananda, in the wisdom of the Tathagata?'

'Even so, Lord!'

'Now why, then, Ananda, dost thou trouble the Tathagata even until the third time?'

'From his own mouth have I heard from the Blessed One, from his own mouth have I received this saying, "Whosoever has thought out, Ananda, and developed, practised" accumulated, and ascended to the very heights of the four paths to saintship, and so mastered them as to be able to use them as a means of mental advancement, and as a basis for edification—he, should he desire it, could remain in the same birth for a kalpa, or for that portion of a kalpa which has yet to run." Now the Tathagata has thought out and thoroughly practised them in all respects as just now fully described, and might, should he desire it, remain alive for a kalpa, or for that portion of a kalpa which has yet to run.'

'Hast thou faith, Ananda?'

'Even so, Lord!'

'Then, O Ananda, thine is the fault, thine is the offence—in that when a suggestion so evident and a hint so clear were thus given thee by the Tathagata, thou was yet incapable of comprehending them, and thou besoughtest the Tathagata, saying , "Vouchsafe, Lord, to remain during the kalpa. Live on, O Blessed One, through the kalpa for the good and the happiness of the great multitudes, out of pity for the world, for the good and the gain and the weal of gods and men." If thou shouldst then have so besought the Tathagata, the Tathagata might have rejected the appeal even to the second time, but the third time he would have granted it. Thine, therefore, O Ananda, is the fault, thine is the offence!

'On one occasion, Ananda, I was dwelling at Rajagaha, on the hill called the Vulture's Peak. Now there, Ananda, I spoke to thee, and said: "How pleasant a spot, Ananda, is Rajagaha; how pleasant is this Vulture's Peak. Whosoever has thought out, Ananda, and developed, practised, accumulated, and ascended to the very heights of the four paths to saintship, and so mastered them as to be able to use them as a means of mental advancement, and as a basis for edification—he, should he desire it, could remain in the same birth for a kalpa, or for that portion of a kalpa which has yet to run. But even when a suggestion so evident and a hint so clear were thus given thee by the Tathagata, thou wast yet incapable of comprehending them, and thou besoughtest not the Tathagata, saying, "Vouchsafe, Lord, to remain during the kalpa. Live on, O Blessed One, through the kalpa for the good and the happiness of the great multitudes, out of pity for the world, for the good and the gain and the weal of gods and men." If thou shouldst then have so besought the Tathagata, the Tathagata might have rejected the appeal even to the second time,but the third time he would have granted it. Thine, therefore, O Ananda, is the fault, thine is the offence!

'On one occasion, Ananda, I was dwelling at that same Rajagaha in the Banyan Grove—on one occasion at that same Rajagaha at the Robbers' Cliff—on one occassion at the same Rajagaha in the Sattapanni Cave on the slope of Mount Vebhara—on one occassion at that same Rajagaha at the Black Rock on the Slope of Mount Isigili—on one occasion at that same Rajagaha in the Sitavana Grove in the mountain cave Sappaasondika—on one occasion at that same Rajagaha in the Tapoda Grove—on one occasion at that same Rajagaha in the Bamboo Grove in the Squirrel's Feeding Ground—on one occasion at that same Rajagaha in Jivaka's Mango Grove—on one occasionat that same Rajagaha in the Deer Forest at Maddakuchchhi.'

'Now there too, Ananda, I spoke to thee, and said: "How pleasant, Ananda, is Rajagaha; how pleasant the Vulture's Peak; how pleasant the Banyan tree of Gotama; how pleasant the Robbers' Cliff; how pleasant the Sattapanni Cave on the slope of Mount Vebhara; how pleasant the Black Rock on the slope of Mount Isigili; how pleasant the mountain cave Sappasondika in the Sitavana Grove; how pleasant the Tapoda Grove; how pleasant the Squirrels' Feeding Ground in the Bamboo Grove; how pleasant Jivaka's Mango Grove; how pleasant the Deer Forest at Maddakuchchhi!

'Whosoever, Ananda, has thought out and developed, practised, accumulated, and ascended to the very heights of the four paths to saintship, and so mastered them so to be able to use them as a means of mental advancement and as a basis for edification—he, should he desire it, could remain in the same birth for a kalpa, or for that portion of a kalpa which has yet to run. Now the Tathagata has thought out and thoroughly practised them in all respects as just now fully described, and might, should he desire it, remain alive for a kalpa, or for that portion of a kalpa which has yet to run.

'On one occasion, Ananda, I was residing here at Vesali at the Udena Chetiya. And there too, Ananda, I spoke to thee and said: "How pleasant, Ananda, is Vesali; how pleasant the Udena Chetiya. Whosoever, Ananda, has thought out and developed, practised, accumulated, and ascended to the very heights of the four paths to saintship, and so mastered them as to be able to use them as a means of mental advancement and as a basis for edification—he, should he desire it, could remain in he same birth for a kalpa, or for that portion of a kalpa which has yet to run. Now the Tathagata has thought out and thoroughly practised them in all respects as just now fully described, and might, should he desire it, remain alive for a kalpa, or for that portion of a kalpa which has yet to run.

'On one occasion, Ananda, I was dwelling here at Vesali at the Gotamaka Chetiya—on one occasion here at Vesali at the Sattamba Chetiya—on one occasion here at Vesali at the Bahuputta Chetiya—on one occasion here at Vesali at the Sarandada Chetiya and on each occasion I spoke to thee, Ananda, in the same words.

'And now to-day, Ananda, at the Chapala Chetiya, I spoke to thee, and said: "How pleasant, Ananda, is Vesali; how pleasant the Udena Chetiya; how pleasant the Gotamaka Chetiya; how pleasant the Sattamba Chetiya; how pleasant the Bahuputta Chetiya; how pelasant the Sarandada Chetiya. Whosoever, Ananda, has thought out and developed, practised, accumulated, and ascended to the very heights of the four paths to saintship, and so mastered them as to be able to use them as a means of mental advancement, and as a basis for edification—he, should he desire it, could remain in the same birth for a kalpa, or for that portion of a kalpa which has yet to run. Now the Tathagata has thought and thoroughly practised them in all respects as just now fully described, and might, should he desire it, remain alive for a kalpa, or for that portion of a kalpa which has yet to run.

'...shall make an end of grief'

'But now, Ananda, have I not formerly declared to you that it is in the very nature of all things, near and dear unto us, that we must divide ourselves from them, leave them, sever ourselves from them? How then, Ananda, can this be possible—whereas anything whatever born, brought into being, and organised, contains within itself the inherent necessity of dissolution—how then can this be possible that such a being should not be dissolved? No such condition can exist. And this mortal being, Ananda, has been relinquished, cast away, renounced, rejected, and abandond by the Tathagata. The remaining sum of life has been surrendered by him. Verily, the word has gone forth from the Tathagata, saying, "The final extinction of the Tathagata shall take place before long. At the end of three months from this time the Tathagata will die!" That the Tathagata for the sake of living should repent him again of that saying—this can no wise be!'

'Come, Ananda, let us go to the Kutagara Hall, to the Mahavana.'

'Even so, Lord!' said the venerable Ananda, in assent, to the Blessed One.

Then the Blessed One proceeded, with Ananda; with him, to the Mahavana to the Kutagara Hall: and when he had arrived there he addressed the venerable Ananda, and said:

'Go now, Ananda, and assemble in the Service Hall such of the brethren as reside in the neighbourhood of Vesali.'

'Even so, Lord,' said the venerable Ananda, in assent, to the Blessed One. And when he had assembled in the Service Hall such of the brethren as resided in the neighbourhood of Vesali, he went to the Blessed One and saluted him and stood beside him. And standing beside him, he addressed the Blessed One, and said:

'Lord! the assembly of the brethren has met together. Let the Blessed One do even as seemeth to him fit.'

Then the Blessed One proceeded to the Service Hall, and sat down there on the mat spread out for him. And when he was seated, the Blessed One addressed the brethren, and said:

'Therefore, O brethren—ye to whom the truths I have perceived have been made known by me—having thoroughly made yourselves masters of them, practise them, meditate upon them, and spread them abroad; in order that pure religion may last long and be perpetuated, in order that it may continue to be for the good and happiness of the great multitudes, out of pity for the world, to the good and the gain and the weal of gods and men!

'Which then, O brethren, are truths which, when I had perceived, I made known to you, which, when you have mastered it behoves you to practise, meditate upon, and spread abroad, in order that pure religion may last long and be perpetuated, in order that it may continue to be for the good and the happiness of the great multitudes out of pity for the world, to the good and the gain and the weal of gods and men?

'They are these:

- The four earnest meditations,
- The fourfold great struggle against sin,
- The four roads to saintship,
- The five moral powers,
- The five organs of spiritual sense,
- The seven kinds of wisdom, and
- The noble eightfold path.

'These, O brethren, are the truths which, when I had perceived, I made known to you, which, when you have mastered it behoves you to practise, meditate upon, and spread abroad, in order that pure religion may last long and be perpetuated, in order that it may continue to be for the good and the happiness of the great multitudes, out of pity for the world, to the good and the gain and the weal of gods and men!'

And the Blessed One exhorted the brethren, and said:

'Behold now, O brethren, I exhort you, saying, "All component things must grow old. Work out your salvation with diligence. The final extinction of the Tathagata will take place before long. At the end of three months from this time the Tathagata will die!"

'My age is now full ripe, my life draws to its close:
I leave you, I depart, relying on myself alone!
Be nearest then, O brethren! holy, full of thought!
Be steadfast in resolve! Keep watch o'er your own hearts!
Who wearies not, but holds fast to this truth and Law,
Shall cross this sea of life, shall make an end of grief.'

Listen to me!

4

The Last Discourses

Now the Blessed One early in the morning robed himself, and taking his bowl, entered Vesali for alms; and when he had passed through Vesali, and had eaten his meal and was returning from his alms-seeking, he gazed at Vesali with an elephant look and addressed the venerable Ananda, and said: 'This will be the last time, Ananda, that the Tathagata will behold Vesali. Come Ananda, let us go on to Bhandagama.'

'Even, so, Lord!' said the venerable Ananda, in assent, to the Blessed One.

And the Blessed One proceeded with a great company of the brethren to Bhandagama; and there the Blessed One stayed in the village itself.

There the Blessed One addressed the brethren, and said: 'It is through not understanding and grasping to four truths, O brethren, that we have had to run so long, to wander so long in this weary path of transmigration—both you and I.

'And what are these four? The noble conduct of life, the noble earnestness in meditation, the noble kind of wisdom, and the noble salvation of freedom. But when noble conduct is realised and known, when noble meditation is realised and known, when noble wisdom is realised and known, when noble freedom is realised and known—then is the craving for existence rooted out, that which leads to renewed existence is destroyed, and there is no more birth.'

Thus spake the Blessed One; and when the Happy One had thus spoken, then again the teacher said:

'Righteousness, earnest thought, wisdom and freedom sublime—
These are the truths realised by Gotama, far-renowned.
Knowing them, he, the knower, proclaimed the truth to the brethren.
The master with eye divine, the quencher of griefs, must die!'

There too, while staying at Bhandagama, the Blessed One held that comprehensive religious discourse with the brethren on the nature of upright conduct, and of earnest contemplation, and of intelligence: 'Great is the fruit, great the advantages of earnest contemplation when set round with upright conduct. Great is the fruit, great the advantage of intellect when set round with earnest contemplation.

'The mind set round with intelligence is freed from the great evils—that is to say, from sensuality, from individuality, from delusion and from ignorance.'

Now when the Blessed One had remained at Bhandagama as long as he desired, he addressed the venerable Ananda, and said: 'Come, Ananda, let us go on to Hatthigama.'

'Even so, Lord!' said Ananda, in assent, to the Blessed One.

Then the Blessed One proceeded with a great company of the brethren to Hatthigama.

And in similar words it is then related how the Blessed One went on to Ambagama, to Jambugama, and to Bhoganagara.

The four references

Now there at Bhoganagara the Blessed One stayed at the Ananda Chetiya.

There the Blessed One addressed the brethren, and said: 'I will teach you, O brethren, these four Great References. Listen thereto, and give good heed, and I will speak.'

'Even so, Lord!' said the brethren, in assent, to the Blessed One, and the Blessed One spake as follows:

'In the first place, brethren, a brother may say thus: "From the mouth of the Blessed One himself have I heard, from his own mouth have I received it. This is the truth, this the Law, this the teaching of the Master." The word spoken, brethren, by that brother should neither be received with praise nor treated with scorn. Without praise and without scorn every word and syllable should be carefully understood, and then put beside the scripture and compared with the rules of the order. If when so compared they do not harmonise with the scripture, and do not fit in with the rules of the order. If when so compared they do not harmonise with the scripture, and do not fit in with the rules of order, then you may come to the conclusion, "Verily, this is not the word of the Blessed One, and has been wrongly grapsed by that brother." Therefore, brethren, you should reject it. But if they harmonise with the scripture and fit in with the rules of the order, then you may come to the conclusion, "Verily, this is the word of the Blessed One and has been well grasped by that brother." This, brethren, you should receive as the first Great Reference.

'Again, brethren, a brother may say thus: "In such and such a dwelling-place there is a company of the brethren with their elders and leaders. From the mouth of that company have I heard, face to face have I received it. This is the truth, this the Law, this the teaching of the Master." The word spoken, brethren, by that brother should neither be received with praise nor treated with scorn. Without praise and without scorn every word and syllable should be carefully understood, and then put beside the scripture and compared with the rules of the order. If when so compared they do not harmonise with the scripture, and do not fit in with the rules of the order, then you may come to the conclusion, "Verily, this is not the word of the Blessed One, and has been wrongly grasped by that company of the brethren." Therefore, brethren, you should reject it. But if they harmonise with the scripture and fit in with the rules of the order, then you may come to the conclusion, "Verily, this is the word of the Blessed One, and has been well grasped by that company of the brethren." This, brethren, you should receive as the second Great Reference.

'Again, brethren, a brother may say thus: "In such and such a dwelling-place there are dwelling many elders of the order, deeply read, holding the faith as handed down by tradition, versed in the truths, versed in the regulations of the order, versed in the summaries of the doctrines and the Law. From the mouth of those elders have I heard, from their mouth have I received it. This is the truth, this the Law, this the teaching of the Master." The word spoken, brethren, by that brother should neither be received with praise nor treated with scorn. Without praise and without scorn every word and syllable should be carefully understood, and then put beside the scripture and compared with the rules of the order. If when so compared they do not harmonise with the scripture, and do not fit in with the rules of the order, then you may come of the conclusion, "Verily, this is not the word of the Blessed One, and has been wrongly grasped by those elders." Therefore, brethren, you should reject it. But if they harmonise with the scripture and fit in with the rules of the order, then you may come to the conclusion, "Verily, this is the word of the Blessed One, and has been well grasped by those elders." This, brethren, you should receive as the third Great Reference.

'Again, brethren, a brother may say, "In such and such a dwelling-place there is living a brother, deeply read, holding the faith as handed down by tradition, versed in the truths, versed in the regulations of the order, versed in the summaries of the doctrines and the Law. From the mouth of that elder have I heard, from his mouth have I received it. This is the truth, this the Law, this the teaching of the Master." The word spoken, brethren, by that brother should neither be received with praise nor treated with scorn. Without praise and without scorn every word and syllable should be carefully understood, and then put beside the scripture and compared with the rules of the order. If when so compared they do not harmonise with the scripture, and do not fit in with the rules of the order, then you may come to the conclusion, "Verily, this is not the word of the Blessed One, and has been wrongly grasped by that brother." Therefore, brethren, you should reject it. But if they harmonise with the scripture and fit in with the rules of the order, then you may come to the conclusion, "Verifly, this is the word of the Blessed One, and has been well grasped by that brother." This, brethren, you should receive as the fourth Great Reference.

'These, brethren, are the Four Great References.'

There, too, the Blessed One held that comprehensive religious talk with the brethren on the nature of upright conduct, and of earnest contemplation, and of intelligence. 'Great is the fruit, great the advantages of earnest contemplation when set round with earnest contemplation. The mind set round with intelligence is freed from the great evils—that is to say, from sensuality, from individuality, from delusion, and from ignorance.'

Now when the Blessed One had remained as long as desired at Bhogagama, he addressed the venerable Ananda, and said: 'Come, Ananda, let us go on to Pava.'

'Even so, Lord!' said the venerable Ananda, in assent, to the Blessed One. And the Blessed One proceeded with a great company of the brethren to Pava.

And there at Pava the Blessed One stayed at the Mango Grove of Chunda, who was by family a smith.

Eats at the smith's home

Now Chunda, the worker in metals, heard that the Blessed One had come to Pava, and was staying there in his Mango Grove.

And Chunda, the worker in metals, went to the place where the Blessed One was, and saluting him took his seat respectfully on one side. And when he was thus seated, the Blessed One instructed, aroused, incited, and gladdened him with religious discourse.

Then he, instructed, aroused, incited and gladdened by the religious discourse, addressed the Blessed One, and said: 'May the Blessed One do me the honour of taking his meal, together with the brethren, at my house to-morrow.'

And the Blessed One signified, by silence, his consent.

Then seeing that the Blessed One had consented, Chunda, the worker in metals, rose from his seat and bowed down before the Blessed One, and keeping him on his right hand as he past him, departed thence.

Now at the end of the night, Chunda, the worker in metals, made ready in his dwelling-place sweet rice and cakes, and a quantity of dried boar's flesh. And he announced the hour to the Blessed One, saying, 'The hour, Lord, has come, and the meal is ready.'

And the Blessed One robed himself early in the morning, and taking his bowl, went with the brethren to the dwelling-place of Chunda, the worker in metals. When he had come thither he seated himself on the seat prepared for him. And when he was seated, he addressed Chunda, the worker in metals, and said: 'As to the dried boar's flesh you have made ready, serve me with it, Chunda; and as to the other food, the sweet rice and cakes, serve the brethren with it.'

'Even so, Lord!' said Chunda, the worker in metals, in assent, to the Blessed One. And the dried boar's flesh he had made ready he served to the Blessed One; whilst the other food, the sweet rice and cakes, he served to the members of the order.

Now the Blessed One addressed Chunda, the worker in metals, and said: 'Whatever dried boar's flesh, Chunda, is left over to thee, that bury in a hole. I see no one, Chunda, on earth nor in Mara's heaven, nor in Brahma's heaven, no one among Samanas and Brahmins, among gods and men, by whom, when he has eaten it, that food can be assimilated, save by the Tathagata.'

'Even so, Lord!' said Chunda, the worker in metals, in assent, to the Blessed One. And whatever dried boar's flesh remained over, that he buried in a hole.

And he went to the place where the Blessed One was; and when he had come there, took his seat respectfully on one side. And when he was seated, the Blessed One instructed and aroused and incited and gladdened Chunda, the worker in metals, with religious discourse. And the Blessed One then rose from his seat and departed thence.

Now when the Blessed One had eaten the food prepared by Chunda, the worker in metals, there fell upon him a dire sickness, the disease of dysentery, and sharp pain came upon him, even unto death. But the Blessed One, mindful and self-possessed, bore it without complaint.

And the Blessed One addressed the venerable Ananda, and said: 'Come, Ananda, let us go on to Kusinara.'

'Even so, Lord!' said the venerable Ananda, in assent, to the Blessed One.

When, he had eaten Chunda's food,
The coppersmith's—thus have I heard—

He bore with fortitude the pain,
The sharp pain even unto death!
And from the dried flesh of the boar, as soon as he had eaten it,
There fell upon the teacher sickness dire,
Then, after nature was relieved the Blessed One announced and said:
'I now am going on to Kusinara.'

'I'm thirsty, Ananda.'

Now the Blessed One went aside from the path to the foot of a certain tree; and when he had come there he addressed the venerable Ananda, and said: 'Fold, I pray you, Ananda, the robe; and spread it out for me. I am weary, Ananda, and must rest awhile!'

'Even so, Lord!' said the venerable Ananda, in assent, to the Blessed One, and spread out the robe folded fourfold.

And the Blessed One seated himself on the seat prepared for him; and when he was seated, he addressed the venerable Ananda, and said: 'Fetch me, I pray you, Ananda, some water. I am thirsty, Ananda, and would drink.'

When he had thus spoken, the venerable Ananda said to the Blessed One: 'But just now, Lord, about five hundred carts have gone over. That water stirred up by the wheels has become shallow and flows fouled and turbid. This river Kakuttha, Lord, not far off, is clear and pleasant, cool and transparent, easy to get down into, and delightful. There the Blessed One may both drink the water, and cool his limbs.'

Again the second time the Blessed One addressed the venerable Ananda, and said: 'Fetch me, I pray you, Ananda, some water. I am thirsty , Ananda, and would drink.'

And again the second time the venerable Ananda said to the Blessed One: 'But just now, Lord, about five hundred carts have gone over. That water stirred up by the wheels has become shallow and flows fouled and turbid. This river Kakuttha, Lord, not far off, is clear and pleasant, cool and transparent, easy to get down into, and delightful. There the Blessed One may both drink the water, and cool his limbs.'

Again the third time the Blessed One addressed the venerable Ananda, and said: 'Fetch me, I pray you, Ananda, some water. I am thirsty, Ananda, and would drink.'

'Even so, Lord!' said the venerable Ananda, in assent, to the Blessed One; and taking a bowl he went down to the streamlet. And to the steramlet which, stirred up by the wheels, was but just now become shallow, and was flowing fouled and turbid, had begun, when the venerable Ananda came up to it, to flow clear and bright and free from all turbidity.

Then Ananda thought: 'How wonderful, how marvellous is the great might and power of the Tathagata! For this streamlet which, stirred up by the wheels, was but just now become shallow and flowing foul and turbid, now, as I come up to it, is flowing clear and bright and free rom all turbidity.'

And taking water in bowl he returned towards the Blessed One; and when he had come where the Blessed One was, he said to him: 'How wonderful, how marvellous is the great might and power of the Tathagata! For this streamlet which, stirred up by the wheels, was but just now become shallow and flowing foul and turbid, now, as I come up to it, is flowing clear and bright and free from all turbidity. Let the Blessed One drink the water! Let the Happy One drink the water!'

Then the Blessed One drank of the water.

'Make me your disciple, sir!'

Now at that time a man named Pukkusa, a young Mallian, a disciple of Alara Kalama's, was passing along the high road from Kusinara to Pava.

And Pukkusa, the young Mallian, saw the Blessed One seated at the foot of a tree. On seeing him, he went up to the place where the Blessed One was, and when he had come there he saluted the Blessed One, and took his rest respectfully on one side. And when he was seated, Pukkusa, the yound Mallian, said to the Blessed One: 'How wonderful a thing is it, Lord! and how marvellous, that those who have gone forth out of the world should pass their time in a state of mind so calm!

'Formerly, Lord, Alama Kalama was once walking along the high road, he sat himself down under a certain tree to rest during the heat of the day. Now, Lord, five hundred carts passed by one after the other, each close to Alara Kalama. And a certain man, who was following close behind that caravan of carts, went up to the place where Alara Kalama was, and when he was come there, he spake as follows to Alara Kalama:

- "But, Lord, did you see those five hundred carts go by?"
- "No, indeed, sir, I saw them not."
- "But, Lord, did you hear the sound of them?"
- "No, indeed, sir, I heard not their sound."
- "But, Lord, were you then asleep?"
- "No, sir, I was not asleep."
- "But, Lord, were you conscious?"
- "Yes, I was conscious, sir."
- "So that you, Lord, though you were both conscious and awake, neither saw, nor heard the sound of

five hundred carts passing by, one after the other, and each close to you. Why, Lord, even your robe was sprinkled over with the dust of them!"

• "It is even so, sir."

"Then thought that man: "How wonderful a thing is it, and how marvellous, that those who have gone forth out of the world should pass their time in a state of mind so calm! So much so that a man though being both conscious and awake, neither sees, nor hears the sound of five hundred carts passing by, one after the other, and each close to him."

'And after giving utterance to his deep faith in Alara Kalama, he departed thence.'

'Now what think you, Pukkusa, which is the more difficult thing either to do or to meet with—that a man being conscious and awake should neither see, nor hear the sound of five hundred carts passing by, one after the other, close to him,—or that a man, being conscious and awake, should neither see, nor hear the sound thereof when the falling rain goes on beating and splashing, and the lightnings are flashing forth, and the thunderbolts are crashing?'

'What in comparison, Lord, can these five hundred carts do, or six or seven or eight or nine or ten hundred, yea, even hundreds and thousands of carts. That certainly is more difficult, both to do and to meet with, that a man being conscious and awake should neither see, nor hear the sounds thereof when the falling rain goes on beating and splashing, and the lightnings are flashing forth, and the thunderbolts are crashing.'

'Now on one occasion, Pukkusa, I was dwelling at Atuma, and was at the Threshing-floor. And at that time the falling rain begun to beat and to splash, and the lightnings to flash forth, and the thunderbolts to crash; and two peasants, brothers, and four oxen were killed.

Then, Pukkusa, a great multitude of people went forth from Atuma, and went up to the place where the two peasants, brothers, and the four oxen, lay killed.

'Now at that time, Pukkusa, I had gone forth from the Threshing-floor, and was walking up and down thinking at the entrance to the Threshing-floor. And a certain man came, Pukkusa, out of that great multitude of people, up to the place where I was; and when he came up he saluted me, and took his place respectfully on one side.

'And as he stood there, Pukkusa, I said to the man:

'"Why then, sir, is this great multitude of people assembled together?"

'"But just now, the falling rain began to beat and to splash, and the lightnings to flash forth, and the thunderbolts to crash; and two peasants, brothers, were killed, and four oxen. Therefore is this great multitude of people gathered together. But where, Lord, were you?"

'"I, sir, have been here all the while."

'"But, Lord, did you see it?"

'"I, sir, saw nothing."

'"But, Lord, did you hear it?"

'"I, sir, heard nothing."

'"Were you then, Lord, asleep?"

'"I, sir, was not asleep."

'"Were you then conscious, Lord?"

'"Even so, sir."

"So that you, Lord, being conscious and awake, neither saw, nor heard the sound thereof when the falling rain went on beating and splashing, and the lightnings were flashing forth, and the thunderbolts were crashing."

"That is so, sir."

'Then, Pukkusa, the thought occurred to that man:

"How wonderful a thing is it, and marvellous that those who have gone forth out of the world should pass their time in a state of mind so calm!—so that a man being conscious and awake neither sees nor hears the sound thereof when the falling rain is beating and splashing, and the lightnings are flashing forth, and the thunderbolts are crashing." And after giving utterance to his deep faith in me, he departed from me with the customary demonstrations of respect.'

And when he had thus spoken, Pukkusa, the young Mallian, addressed the Blessed One in these words: 'Now I, Lord, as to the faith that I had in Alara Kalama, that I winnow away as in a mighty wind, and wash it away as in a swiftly running stream. Most excellent, Lord, are the words of thy mouth, most excellent! Just as if a man were to set up that which is thrown down, or were to reveal that which is hidden away, or were to point out the right road to him who has gone astray, or were to bring a lamp into the darkness, so that those who have eyes can see external forms—just even so, Lord, has the truth been made known to me, in many a figure, by the Blessed One. And I, even I, betake myself, Lord, to the Blessed One as my refuge, to the Truth, and to the Brotherhood. May the Blessed One accept me as a disciple, as a true believer, from this day forth, as long as life endures!'

Now Pukkusa, the young Mallian, addressed a certain man, and said. 'Fetch me, I pray you, my good man, a pair of robes of cloth of gold, burnished and ready for wear.'

'So be it, sir!' said that man, in assent, to Pukkusa, the young Mallian; and he brought a pair of robes of cloth of gold, burnished and ready for wear.

And the Mallian Pukkusa presented the pair of robes of cloth of gold, burnished and ready for wear, to the Blessed One, saying 'Lord, this pair of robes of burnished cloth of gold is ready for wear. May the Blessed One show me favour and accept it at may hands!'

'In that case, Pukkusa, robe me in one, and Ananda in one.'

Avalokiteswara Buddha

'Even so, Lord!' said Pukkusa, in assent, to the Blessed One; and in one he robed the Blessed One, and in one, Ananda.

Then the Blessed One instructed and aroused and incited and gladdened Pukkusa, the young Mallian, with religious discourse. And Pukkusa, the young Mallian, when he had been instructed and aroused and incited and gladdened by the Blessed One with religious discourse, arose from his seat, and bowed down before the Blessed One; and keeping him on his right hand as he past him, departed thence.

Now not long after the Mallian Pukkusa had gone, the venerable Ananda placed that pair of robes of cloth of gold, burnished and ready for wear, on the body of the Blessed One, and when it was so placed on the body of the Blessed One, it appeared to have lost its splendour!

And the venerable Ananda said to the Blessed One: 'How wonderful a thing is it, Lord, and how marvellous, that the colour of the skin of the Blessed One should be so clear, so exceeding bright! For when I placed even this pair of robes of burnished cloth of gold and ready for wear on the body of the Blessed One, lo! it seemed as if it had lost its splendour!'

'It is even so, Ananda. Ananda, there are two occasions on which the colour of the skin of a Tathagata becomes clear and exceeding bright. What are the two?

'On the night, Ananda, on which a Tathagata attains to the supreme and perfect insight, and on the night in which he passes finally away, in that utter passing away which leaves nothing whatever to remain—on these two occasions the colour of the skin of the Tathagata becomes clear and exceeding bright.

'And now this day, Ananda, at the third watch of the night, in the Upavattana of Kusinara, in the Sala Grove of the Mallians, between the twin Sala tress, the utter passing away of the Tathagata will take place. Come, Ananda, let us go on to the river Kakuttha.'

'Even, so, Lord!' said the venerable Ananda, in assent, to the Blessed One.

The pair of robes of cloth of gold,
All burnished, Pukkusa had brought,
Clad on with them the Master then
Shone forth in colour like to gold!

At the river Kakuttha

Now the Blessed One with a great company of the brethren went on to the river Kakuttha; and when he had come there, he went down into the water, and bathed, and drank. And coming up out again on the other side, he went on to the Mango Grove.

And when he was come there, he addressed the venerable Chundaka, and said: 'Fold, I pray you Chundaka, a robe in four and spread it out. I am weary, Chundaka, and would lie down.'

'Even so, Lord!' said the venerable Chundaka, in assent, to the Blessed One. And he folded a robe in four, and spread it out.

And the Blessed One laid himself down on his right side, with one foot resting on the other; and calm and self-possessed, he meditated on the idea of rising up again in due time. And the venerable Chundaka seated himself there in front of the Blessed One.

The Buddha to Kakuttha's river came,
Whose clear and pleasant limpid flow,
He plunged beneath the stream wearied and worn,
The Buddha without equal in the world!
When he had bathed and drunk, the teacher then
Crossed o'er, the brethren thronging round his steps;
The Blessed Master, preaching the while the truth,
The Mighty Sage came to the Mango Grove.

There spake he to the brother Chundaka:
'Spread me the fourfold robe out as a couch.'
Cheered by the Holy One, he quickly spread
The fourfold robe in order on the ground.
The Master laid him down, wearied and worn;
And there, before him, Chunda took his seat.

And the Blessed One addressed the venerable Ananda, and said: 'Now it may happen, Ananda, that some one should stir up remorse in Chunda the smith, by saying, "This is evil to thee, Chunda, and loss to thee in that when the Tathagata had eaten his last meal from thy provision, then he died." Any such remorse, Ananda, in Chunda the smith should be checked by saying, "**This is good to thee, Chunda, and gain to thee in that when the Tathagata had eaten his last meal from thy provision, then he died.** From the very month of the Blessed One, Chunda, have I heard, from his own mouth have I received this saying, 'These two offerings of food are of equal fruit, and of equal profit, and of much greater fruit and much greater profit than any other—and which are the two? **The offering of food which, when a Tathagata has eaten, he attains to supreme and perfect insight; and the offering of food which, when a Tathagata has eaten, he passes away by that utter passing away in which nothing whatever remains behind—these two offerings of food are of equal fruit and of equal profit, and of much greater fruit and much greater profit than any others.** There has been laid up by Chunda the smith a karma redounding to length of life, redounding to good birth, redounding to good fortune, redounding to good fame, redounding to the inheritance of heaven, and of sovereign power." In this way, Ananda, should be checked any remorse in Chunda the smith.'

Then the Blessed One perceiving how the matter stood, uttered, even at that time, this hymn of exultation:

'To him who gives shall virtue be increased;
In him who curbs himself, no anger can arise;
The righteous man casts of all sinfulness,
And by the rooting out of lust, and bitterness,
And all delusion, doth to Nirvana reach!'

5

Prepares to Pass Away

Now the Blessed One addressed the venerable Ananda, and said: 'Come, Ananda, let us go on to the Sala Grove of the Mallas, the Upavattana of Kusinara, on the further side of the river Hiranyavati.'

'Even so, Lord!' said the venerable Ananda, in assent, to the Blessed One.

And the Blessed One proceeded with a great company of the brethren to the Sala Grove of the Mallas, the Upavattana of Kusinara, on the further side of the river Hiranyavati; and when he had come there he addressed the venerable Ananda, and said:

'Spread over for me, I pray you, Ananda, the couch with its head to the north, between the twin Sala trees. I am weary, Ananda, and would lie down.'

'Even so, Lord!' said the venerable Ananda, in assent, to the Blessed One. And he spread a covering over the couch with its head to the north, between the twin Sala trees. And the Blessed One laid himself down on his right side, with one leg resting on the other; and he was mindful and self-possessed.

Now at that time the twin Sala trees were all one mass of bloom with flowers out of season; and all over the body of the Tathagata these dropped and sprinkled and scattered themselves, out of reverence for the successor of the

Buddhas of old. And heavenly Mandarava flowers, too, and heavenly sandalwood powder came falling from the sky, and all over the body of the Tathagata they descended and sprinkled and scattered themselves, out of reverence for the successor of the Buddhas of old. And heavenly music was sounded in the sky, out of reverence for the successor of the Buddhas of old. And heavenly songs came wafted from the skies, out of reverence for the successor of the Buddhas of old!

Then the Blessed One addressed the venerable Ananda, and said: 'The twin Sala trees are all one mass of bloom with flowers out of season; all over the body of the Tathagata these drop and sprinkle and scatter themselves, out of reverence for the successor of the Buddhas of old. And heavenly Mandarava flowers, too, and heavenly Sandalwood powder come falling from the sky, and all over the body of the Tathagata they descend and sprinkle and scatter themselves, out of reverence for the successor of the Buddhas of old. And heavenly music sounds in the sky, out of reverence for the successor of the Buddhas of old. And heavenly songs come wafted from the skies, out of reverence for the successor of the Buddhas of old!

'Now it is not thus, Ananda, that the Tathagata is rightly honoured, reverenced, venerated, held sacred or revered. But the brother or the sister, the devout man or the devout woman, who continually fulfils all the greater and the lesser duties, who is correct in life, walking according to the precepts—it is he who rightly honours, reverences, generates, holds sacred, and reveres the Tathagata with the worthiest homage. Therefore, O Ananda, be ye constant in the fulfilment of the greater and of the lesser duties, and be ye correct in life, walking according to the precepts; and thus, Ananda, should it be taught.'

Now at that time the venerabie Upavana was standing in front of the Blessed One, fanning him. And the Blessed

One was not pleased with Upavana, and he said to him: 'Stand aside, O brother, stand not in front of me!'

Then this thought sprung up in the mind of the venerable Ananda: 'The venerable Upavana has long been in close personal attendance and service on the Blessed One. And now, at the last moment, the Blessed One is not pleased with Upavana, and has said to him, "Stand aside, O brother, stand not in front of me !" What may be the cause and what the reason that the Blessed One is not pleased with Upavana, and speaks thus with him?'

And the venerable Ananda said to the Blessed One: 'The venerable Upavana has long been in close personal attendance and service on the Blessed One. And now, at the last moment, the Blessed One is not pleased with Upavana, and has said to him, "Stand aside, O brother, stand not in front of me!" What may be the cause and what the reason that the Blessed One is not pleased with Upavana, and speaks thus with him?'

'Spirits want to see me passing away.'

'In great numbers, Ananda, are the gods of the ten world-systems assembled together to behold the Tathagata. For twelve leagues, Ananda, around the Sala Grove of the Mallas, the Upavattana of Kusinara, there is no spot in size even as the pricking of the point of the tip of a hair which is not pervaded by powerful spirits. And the spirits, Ananda, are murmuring, and saying, "From afar have we come to behold the Tathagata. Few and far between are the Tathagatas, the Arahat Buddhas, who appear in the world; and now to-day, in the last watch of the night, the death of a Tathagata will take place; and this eminent brother stands in front of the Tathagata, concealing him, and in his last hour we are prevented from beholding the Tathagata;" thus, Ananda. do the spirits murmur.'

'But of what kind of spirits is the Blessed One thinking?'

'There are spirits, Ananda, in the sky, but of worldly mind, who dishevel their hair and weep, who stretch forth their arms and weep, who fall prostrate on the ground, and roll to and fro in anguish at the thought: "Too soon will the Blessed One die! Too soon will the Happy One pass away! Too soon will the Light of the World vanish away!"'

'There are spirits, too, Ananda, on the earth, and of worldly mind, who tear their hair and weep, who stretch forth their arms and weep, who fall prostrate on the ground, and roll to and fro in anguish at the thought: "Too soon will the Blessed One die! Too soon will the Happy One pass away! Full soon will the Eye of the world disappear from sight!"

'But the spirits who are free from passion bear it, calm and self-possessed, mindful of the saying which begins, "Impermanent indeed are all component things. How then is it possible whereas anything whatever, when born, brought into being, and organised, contains within itself the inherent necessity of dissolution—how then is it possible that such a being should not be dissolved? No such condition can exist!'

'In times past, Lord, the brethren, when they had spent the rainy season in different districts, used to come to see the Tathagata, and we used to receive those very reverend brethren to audience, and to wait upon the Blessed One. But, Lord, after the end of the Blessed One, we shall not be able to receive those very reverend brethren to audience, and to wait upon the Blessed One.'

The four places

'There are these four places, Ananda, which the believing man should visit with feelings of reverence and awe. Which are the four?

'The place, Ananda, at which the believing man can say, "Here the Tathagata was born!" is a spot to be visited with feelings of reverence and awe.

'The place, Ananda, at which the believing man can say, "Here the Tathagata attained to the supreme and perfect insight!" is a spot to be visited with feelings of reverence and awe.

'The place, Ananda, at which the believing man can say, "Here was the kingdom of righteousness set on foot by the Tathagata!" is a spot to be visited with feelings of reverence and awe.

'The place, Ananda, at which the believing man can say, "Here the Tathagata passed finally away in that utter passing away which leaves nothing whatever to remain behind!" is a spot to be visited with feelings of reverence and awe.

'And there will come, Ananda, to such spots, believers, brethren and sisters of the order, or devout men and devout women, and will say, "Here was the Tathagata born!" or, "Here did the Tathagata attain to the supreme and perfect insight!" or, "Here was the kingdom of righteousness set on foot by the Tathagata!" or, "Here the Tathagata passed away in that utter passing away which leaves nothing whatever to remain behind!"

'And they, Ananda, who shall die while they, with believing heart, are journeying on such pilgrimage, shall be reborn after death, when the body shall dissolve, in the happy realms of heaven.'

'How are we to conduct ourselves, Lord, with regard to womankind?'

'Don't see them, Ananda.'

'But if we should see them, what are we to do?'

'Abstain from speech, Ananda.'

'But if they should speak to us, Lord, what are we to do?'

'Keep wide awake, Ananda.'

I'm coming!

About the remains

'What are we to do, Lord, with the remains of the Tathagata?'

'Hinder not, yourselves, Ananda, by honouring the remains of the Tathagata. Be zealous, I beseech you, Ananda, in your own behalf! Devote yourselves to your own good! Be earnest, be zealous, be intent on your own good! There are wise men, Ananda, among the nobles, among the Brahmins, among the heads of houses, who are firm believers in the Tathagata; and they will do due honour to the remains of the Tathagata.'

'What should be done, Lord, with the remains of the Tathagata!'

'As men treat the remains of a king of kings, so, Ananda, should they treat the remains of a Tathagata.'

'And how, Lord, do they treat the remains of a king of kings?'

'They wrap the body of a king of kings, Ananda, in a new cloth. When that is done, they wrap it in carded cotton wool. When that is done, they wrap it in a new cloth,—and so on till they have wrapped the body in five hundred successive layers of both kinds. Then they place the body in an oil vessel of iron, and cover that close up with another oil vessel of iron. They then build a funeral pile of all kinds of perfumes, and burn the body of the king of kings. And then at the four crossroads they erect a dagaba to the king of kings. This, Ananda, is the way in which they treat the remains of a king of kings.

'And as they treat the remains of a king of kings, so, Ananda, should they treat the remains of the Tathagata. At the four crossroads a dagaba should be erected to the Tathagata. And whosoever shall there place garlands or perfumes or paint, or make salutations there, or become in its presence calm in heart—that shall long be to them for a profit and a joy.

'These men, Ananda, worthy of a dagaba, are four in number. Which are the four?'

'A Tathagata, or Arahat-Buddha, is worthy of a dagaba. A Pachcheka-Buddha is worthy ota dagaba.

'A true hearer of the Tathagata is worthy of a dagaba. A king of kings is worthy of a dagaba.

'And on account of what circumstance, Ananda, is a Tathagata, an Arahat-Buddha, worthy of a dagaba?

'At the thought, Ananda, "This is the dagaba of that Blessed One, of that Arahat-Buddha," the hearts of many shall be made calm and happy; and since they there had calmed and satisfied their hearts they will be reborn after death, when the body has dissolved, in the happy realms of heaven. It is on account of this circumstance, Ananda, that a Tathagata, an Arahat-Buddha, is worthy of a dagaba.

'And on account of what circumstance, Ananda, is a Pachcheka-Buddha worthy of a dagaba?

'At the thought, Ananda, "This is the dagaba of that Blessed One, of that Pachcheka-Buddha," the hearts of many shall be made calm and happy; and since they there had calmed and satisfied their hearts they will be reborn after death, when the body has dissolved, in the happy realms of heaven. It is on account of this circumstance, Ananda, that a Pachcheka-Buddha is worthy of a dagaba.

'And on account of what circumstance, Ananda, is a true hearer of the Blessed One, the Arahat-Buddha, worthy of a dagaba?

'At the thought. Ananda, "This is the dagaba of that true hearer of the Blessed Arahat-Buddha," the hearts of many shall be made calm and happy; and since they there had calmed and satisfied their hearts they will be reborn after death, when the body has dissolved, in the happy realms of heaven. It is on account of this circumstance, Ananda, that a true hearer of the Blessed One, the Arahat-Buddha, is worthy of a dagaba.

'And on account of what circumstance, Ananda, is a king of kings worthy of a dagaba?

'At the thought, Ananda, " This is the dagaba of that righteous king who ruled in righteousness," the hearts of many shall be made calm and happy; and since they there had calmed and satisfied their hearts they will be reborn after death, when the body has dissolved, in the happy realms of heaven. It is on account of this circumstance, Ananda, that a king of kings is worthy of a dagaba,

'These four, Ananda, are the persons worthy of a dagaba.'

Ananda weeps

Now the venerable Ananda went into the Vihara, and stood leaning against the lintel of the door, and weeping at the thought: "Alas! I remain still but a learner, one who has yet to work out his own perfection. And the Master is about to pass away from me—he who is so kind!"

Now the Blessed One called the brethren, and said: 'Where, then, brethren, is Ananda?'

'The venerable Ananda, Lord, has gone into the Vihara, and stands leaning against the lintel of the door, and weeping at the thought: "Alas! I remain still but a learner, one who has yet to work out his own perfection. And the Master is about to pass away from me—he who is so kind!"'

And the Blessed One called a certain brother, and said: 'Go now, brother, and call Ananda in my name, and say, "Brother Ananda, the Master calls for thee."

'Even so, Lord!' said that brother, in assent, to the Blessed One. And he went up to the place where the venerable Ananda was; and when he had come there, he said to the venerable Ananda: 'Brother Ananda, the Master calls for thee.'

'Very well, brother,' said the venerable Ananda, in assent, to that brother. And he went up to the place where the Blessed One was, and when he had come there, he bowed down before the Blessed One, and took his seat respectfully on one side.

Then the Blessed One said to the venerable Ananda, as he sat there by his side: 'Enough, Ananda! Do not let yourself be troubled; do not weep! Have I not already, on former occasions, told you that it is in the very nature of all things most near and dear unto us that we must divide ourselves from them, leave them, sever ourselves from them? How, then, Ananda, can this be possible—whereas anything whatever born, brought into being, and organised, contains within itself the inherent necessity of dissolution—how, then, can this be possible, that such a being should not be dissolved? No such condition can exist! For a long time, Ananda, have you been very near to me by acts of love, kind and good, that never varies, and is beyond all measure. For a long time, Ananda, have you been very near to me by words of love, kind and good, that never varies, and is beyond all measure. For a long time, Ananda, have you been very near to me by thoughts of love, kind and good, that never varies, and is beyond all measure. You have done well, Ananda! Be earnest in effort, and you too shall soon be free from the great evils—from sensuality, from individuality, from delusion, and from ignorance!'

The qualities of Ananda

Then the Blessed One addressed the brethren, and said: 'Whosoever, brethren, have been Arahat-Buddhas through the long ages of the past, there were servitors just as devoted to those Blessed Ones as Ananda has been to me. And whosoever, brethren, shall be Arahat- Buddhas in the long ages of the future, there shall be servitors just as devoted to those Blessed Ones as Ananda has been to me.

'He is a wise man, brethren, is Ananda. He knows when it is the right time for him to come and visit the Tathagata, and when it is the right time for the brethren and sisters of the order for devout men and devout women, for a king, or for a king's ministers, for other teachers or their disciples, to come and visit the Tathagata.

'Brethren, there are these four wonderful and marvellous qualities in Ananda. Which are the four?

'Brethren, there are these four wonderful nad marvellous qualities in Ananda. Which are the four?

'If, brethren, a number of the brethren of the order should come to visit Ananda, they are filled with joy beholding him; and if Ananda should then preach the truth to them, they are filled with joy at the discourse; while the company of brethren is ill at ease, brethren, when Ananda is silent.

'If, brethren, a number of the sisters of the order, or of devout men, or of devout women, should come to visit Ananda, they are filled with joy on beholding him; and if Ananda should then preach the truth to them, they are filled with joy at the discourse; while the company of sisters is ill at ease, brethren, when Ananda is silent.

'Brethren, there are these four wonderful and marvellous qualities in a king of kings. What are the four?'

'If, brethren, a number of nobles, or Brahmin, or heads of houses, or Samanas should come to visit a king of kings, they are filled with joy on beholding him; and if the king of kings should then speak, they are filled with joy at what is said; while they are ill at ease, brethren, when the king of kings is silent.

'Just so, brethren, are the four wonderful and marvellous qualities in Ananda.

'If, brethren, a number of the brethren of the order, or of the sisters of the order, or of devout men, or of devout women, should come to visit Ananda, they are filled with joy on beholding him; and if Ananda should then preach the truth to them, they are filled with joy at the discourse;

while the company of brethren is ill at ease, brethren, when Ananda is silent.

'Now these, brethren, are the four wonderful and marvellous qualities that are in Ananda.'

When he had thus spoken the venerable Ananda, said to the Blessed One:

'Let not the Blessed One die in this little wattel and daub town, in this town in the midst of the jungle, in this branch township. For, Lord, there are other great cities, such as Champa, Rajagaha, Savatthi, Saketa, Kosambi, and Benares. Let the Blessed One die in one of them. There are many wealthy nobles and Brahmins and heads of houses, believers in the Tathagata, who will pay due honour to the remains of the Tathagata.'

'Say not so, Ananda! Say not so, Ananda, that this is but a small wattel and daub town, a town in the midst of the jungle, a branch township. Long ago, Ananda, there was a king, by name Maha-Sudassana, a king of kings, a righteous man who ruled in righteousness, Lord of the four quarters of the earth, conqueror, protector of his people, possessor of the seven royal treasures. This Kusinara, Ananda, was the royal city of king Maha-Sudassana, under the name of Kusavati, and on the east and on the west it was twelve leagues in length, and on the north and on the south it was seven leagues in breadth.

'That royal city Kusavati, Ananda, was mighty, and prosperous, and full of people, crowded with men, and provided with all things for food. Just, Ananda, as the royal city of the gods, Alakananda by name, is mighty, prosperous, and full of people, crowded with the gods and provided with all kinds of food, so, Ananda, was the royal city Kusavati, mighty and prosperous, full of people, crowded with men, and provided with all kinds of food.

'Both by day and by night, Ananda, the royal city Kusavati resounded with the ten cries; that is to say, the noise of elephants, and the noise of horses, and the noise of chariots; the sounds of the drum, of the tabor, and of the lute; the sound of singing, and the sounds of the cymbal and of the gong; and lastly, with the cry, "Eat, drink, and be merry!"

'Go now, Ananda, and enter into Kusinara, and inform the Mallas of Kusinara, saying, "This day, O Vasetthas, in the last watch of the night, the final passing away of the Tathagata will take place. Be favourable herein, O Vasetthas, be favourable. Give no occasion to reproach yourselves hereafter, saying, "In our own village did the death of our Tathagata take place, and we took not the opportunity of visiting the Tathagata in his last hours."

'Even so, Lord,' said the venerable Ananda, in assent, to the Blessed One; and he robed himself, and taking his bowl, entered into Kusinara attended by another member of the order.

Ananda goes to Kusinara

Now at that time the Mallas of Kusinara were assembled in the council hall on some public affair.

And the venerable Ananda went to the council hall of the Mallas of Kusinara; and when he had arrived there, he informed them, saying, 'This day, O Vasetthas, in the last watch of the night, the final passing away of the Tathagata will take place. Be favourable herein, O Vasetthas, be favourable. Give no occasion to reproach yourselves hereafter, saying, "In our own village did the death of our Tathagata take place, and we took not the opportunity of visiting the Tathagata in his last hours."'

And when they had heard this saying of the venerable Ananda, the Mallas with their young men and maidens and their wives were grieved, and sad, and afflicted at heart. And some of them wept, dishevelling their hair, and stretched forth their arms and wept, fell prostrate on the ground, and rolled to and fro in anguish at the thought: 'Too soon will the Blessed One die! Too soon will the Happy One pass away! Too soon will the Light of the World vanish away!'

Then the Mallas, with their young men and maidens and their wives, being grieved and sad and afflicted at heart, went to the Sala Grove of the Mallas, to the Upavattana, and to the place where the venerable Ananda was.

Then the venerable Ananda thought: 'If I allow the Mallas of Kusinara, one by one, to pay their respects to the Blessed One, the whole of the Mallas of Kusinara will not have been presented to the Blessed One until this night brightens up into the dawn. Let me, now cause the Mallas of Kusinara to stand in groups, each family in a group, and so present them to the Blessed One, saying, "Lord! a Malla of such and such a name, with his children, his wives, his retinue, and his friends, humbly bows down at the feet of the Blessed One."'

And the venerable Ananda caused the Mallas of Kusinara to stand in groups, each family in a group, and so presented them to the Blessed One, and said: 'Lord! a Malla of such and such a name, with his children, his wives, his retinue, and his friends, humbly bows down at the feet of the Blessed One.'

And after this manner the venerable Ananda presented all the Mallas of Kusinara to the Blessed One in the first watch of the night.

Now at that time a mendicant named Subhadda, who not a believer, was dwelling at Kusinara. And the mendicant Subhadda heard the news: 'This very day, they say, in the third watch of the night, will take place the final passing away of the Samana Gotama.'

Then thought the mendicant Subhadda: 'This have I heard from fellow mendicants of mine, old and well stricken in years, teachers and disciples, when they said: "Sometimes and seldom do Tathagatas appear in the world, the Arahat Buddhas." Yet this day, in the last watch of the night, the final passing away of the Samana Gotama will take place. Now a certain feeling of uncertainty has sprung up in my mind; and this faith have I in the Samana Gotama, that he, methinks, is able so to present the truth that I may get rid of this feeling of uncertainty.'

Then the mendicant Subhadda went to the Sala Grove of the Mallas, to the Upavattana of Kusinara, to the place where the venerable Ananda was.

And when he had come there he said to the venerable Ananda: 'Thus have I heard from fellow mendicants of mine, old and well stricken in years, teachers and disciples, when they said: "Sometimes and seldom do Tathagatas appear in the world, the Arahat Buddhas." Yet this day, in the last watch of the night, the final passing away of the Samana Gotama will take place. Now a certain feeling of uncertainty has sprung up in my mind; and this faith have I in Samana Gotama, that he, rnethinks, is able so to present the truth that I may get rid of this feeling of uncertainty. See that I, even I, Ananda, might be allowed to see the Samana Gotama!'

And when he had thus spoken the venerable Ananda said to the mendicant Subhadda: 'Enough! friend Subhadda. Trouble not the Tathagata. The Blessed One is weary.'

And again the mendicant Subhadda made the same request in the same words, and received the same reply; and the third time the mendicant Subhadda made the same request in the same words, and received the same reply.

Now the Blessed One overheard this conversation of the venerable Ananda with the mendicant Subhadda. And the Blessed One called the venerable Ananda, and said: 'It is enough, Ananda! Do not keep out Subhadda. Subhadda,

Ananda, may be allowed to see the Tathagata. Whatever Subhadda may ask of me, he will ask from a desire for knowledge, and not to annoy me. And whatever I may say in answer to his questions, that he will quickly understand.'

Then the venerable Ananda said to Subhadda, the mendicant; 'Enter in, friend Subhadda; for the Blessed One gives you leave.'

Subhadda becomes the last disciple

Then Subhadda, the mendicant, went in to the place where the Blessed One was, and saluted him courteously, and after exchanging with him the compliments of esteem and of civility, he took his seat on one side. And when he was thus seated, Subhadda, tbe mendicant, said to the Blessed One: 'The Brahmins by saintliness of life, Gotama, who are heads of companies of disciples and students, teachers of students, well known, renowned, founders of schools of doctrine, esteemed as good men by the multitude—to wit, Purana Kassapa, Makkhali of the cattle-pen, Ajita of the garment of hair, Kachchayana of the Pakudha tree, Sanjaya the son of the Belatthi slave-girl, and Nigantha of the Natha clan—have they all, according to their own assertion, thoroughly understood things? or have they not? or are there some of them who have understood, and some who have not?'

'Enough, Subhadda! Let this matter rest whether they, according to their own assertion, have thoroughly understood things, or whether they have not, or whether some of them have understood and some have not! The truth, Subhadda, will I teach you. Listen well to that, and give ear attentively, and I will speak.'

'Even so, Lord!' said the mendicant Subhadda, in assent, to the Blessed One.

And the Blessed One spake: 'In whatsoever doctrine and discipline, Subhadda, the noble eightfold path is not found, neither in it is there found a man of true saintliness of the first or of the second or of the third or of the fourth degree. And in whatsoever doctrine and discipline, Subhadda, the noble eightfold path is found, is found the man of true saintliness of the first and the second and the third and the fourth degree. Now in this doctrine and discipline, Subhadda, is found the Noble eightfold path, and in it alone, Subhadda, is the man of true saintliness. Void are the systems of other teachers—void of true saints. And in this one, Subhadda, may the brethren live the Life that's Right, so that the world be not bereft of Arahats.

But twenty-nine was I when I renounced
The world, Subhadda, seeking after good.
For fifty years and one year more, Subhadda,
Since I went out, a pilgrim have I been
Through the wide realms of virtue and of truth,
And outside these no reall y "saint" can be!

'Yea, not of the first, nor of the second, nor of the third, nor of the fourth degree. Void are the systems of other teachers—void of true saints. But in this one, Subhadda, may the brethren live the perfect life, that the world be not bereft of those who have reached the highest fruit.'

And when he had thus spoken, Subhadda, the mendicant, said to the Blessed One: 'Most excellent, Lord, are the words of thy mouth, most excellent! Just as if a man were to set up that which is thrown down, or were to reveal that which is hidden away, or were to point out the right road to him who has gone astray, or were to bring a lamp into the darkness, so that those who have eyes can see external forms;—Just even so, Lord, has the truth been made known to me, in many a figure, by the Blessed One. And I, even I, betake myself, Lord, to the Blessed One as my refuge, to the truth, and to the order. May the Blessed One accept me as a disciple, as a true believer, from this day forth, as long as life endures!'

Flying angels

'Whosoever, Subhadda, that has formerly been a follower of another doctrine and then desires to be received into the higher or the lower grade in this doctrine and discipline, he remains on probation for the space of four months; and at the end of the four months, the brethren, exalted in spirit, receive him into the lower or into the higher grade of the order. Nevertheless, in this case I acknowledge the difference in persons.'

'If, Lord, whosoever that has formerly been a follower of another doctrine and then desires to be received into the higher or the lower grade in this doctrine and discipline,—if, in that case, such a person remains on probation for the space of four months; and at the end of the four months, the brethren, exalted in spirit, receive him into the lower or into the higher grade of the order—I too, then, will remain on probation for the space of four months; and at the end of the four months let the brethren, exalted in spirit, receive me into the lower or into the higher grade of the order!'

But the Blessed One called the venerable Ananda, and said: 'As it is, Ananda, receive Subhadda into the order!'

'Even so, Lord!' said the venerable Ananda, in assent, to the Blessed One.

And Subhadda, the mendicant, said to the venerable Ananda: 'Great is your gain, friend Ananda, great is your good fortune, friend Ananda, that you all have been sprinkled with the sprinkling of discipleship in this brotherhood at the hands of the Master himself!'

So Subhadda, the mendicant, was received into the higher grade of the order under the Blessed One; and from immediately after his ordination the venerable Subhadda remained alone and separate, earnest, zealous, and resolved. And e'er long he attained to that supreme goal of the higher life for the sake of which men go out from all and every household gain and comfort to become houseless wanderers—yea, that supreme goal did he, by himself, and while yet in this visible world, bring himself to the knowledge of, and continue to realise, and to see face to face! And he became conscious that birth was at an end, that the higher life had been fulfilled, that all that should be done had been accomplished, and that after this present life there would be no beyond!

So the venerable Subhadda became yet another among the Arahats; and he was the last disciple whom the Blessed One himself converted.

6

Passes into Nirvana

Now the Blessed One addressed the venerable Ananda and said: 'It may be, Ananda, that in some of you the thought may arise: "The word of the Master is ended, we have no teacher more!" But it is not thus, Ananda, that you should regard it. The truths and the rules of the order which I have set forth and laid down for you all, let them, after I am gone, be the Teacher to you,

'Ananda! when I am gone, address not one another in the way in which the brethren have heretofore addressed each other—with the epithet, that is of "Avuso" (Friend). A younger brother may be addressed by an elder with his name, or his family name, or the title "Friend." But an elder should be addressed by a younger brother as "Lord" or as "Venerable Sir."

'When I am gone, Ananda, let the order, if it should so wish, abolish all lesser and minor precepts.

'When I am gone, Ananda, let the higher penalty be imposed on brother Chhanna.'

'But what, Lord, is the higher penalty?'

'Let Chhanna say whatever he may like, Ananda, the brethren should neither speak to him, nor exhort him, nor admonish him.'

Enquire freely

Then the Blessed One addressed the brethren, and said: 'It may be, brethren, that there may be doubt or misgiving in the mind of some brother as to the Buddha, or the truth, or the path, or the way. Enquire, brethern, freely. Do not have to reproach yourselves afterwards with the thought "Our teacher was face to face with us, and we could not bring ourselves to enquire of the Blessed One when we were face to face with him."

And when he had thus spoken the brethren were silent.

Then the Blessed One addressed the brethren, and said: 'It may be, brethren, that you put no questions out of reverence for the teacher. Let one friend communicate to another.'

And even this time the brethren were silent.

And the venerable Ananda said to the Blessed One: 'How wonderful a thing is it, Lord, and how marvellous! Verily, I believe that in this whole assembly of the brethren, there is not one brother who has any doubt or misgiving as to the Buddha, or the truth, or the path, or the way!'

'It is out of the fulness of faith that thou hast spoken, Ananda! But, Ananda, the Tathagata knows for certain that in this whole assembly of the brethren there is not one brother who has any doubt or misgiving as to the Buddha, or the truth, or the parth, or the way! For even the most backward, Ananda, of all these five hundred brethren has become converted, and is no longer liable to be born in a state of suffering, and is assured of final salvation.'

The last word

Then the Blessed One addressed the brethren, and said, 'Behold now, brethren, I exhort you, saying, "**Decay is inherent in all component things! Work out your salvation with diligence!**"

This was the last word of the Tathagata!

Passing into infinity

Then the Blessed One entered into the first stage of deep meditation. And rising out of the first stage he passed into the second. And rising out of the second he passed into the third. And rising out of the third stage he passed into the fourth. And rising out of the fourth stage of deep meditation be entered into the state of mind to which the infinity of space is alone present. And passing out of the mere consciousness of the infinity of thought he entered into a state of mind to which nothing at all was specially present. And passing out of the consciousness of no special object he fell into a state between consciousness and unconsciousness. And passing out of the state between consciousness and unconsciousness, he fell into a state in which the consciousness both of sensations and of ideas had wholly passed away.

Then the venerable Ananda said to the venerable Anuruddha: 'O my Lord, O Anuruddha, the Blessed One is dead!'

'Nay! brother Ananda, the Blessed One is not dead. He has entered into that state in which both sensations and ideas have ceased to be!'

Then the Blessed One passing out of the state in which both sensations and ideas have ceased to be, entered into the state between consciousness and unconsciousness. And passing out of the state between consciousness and unconsciousness he entered into the state of mind to which nothing at all is specially present. And passing out of the consciousness of no special object he entered into the state of mind to which the infinity of thought is alone present. And passing out of the mere consciousness of the infinity of thought he entered into the state of mind to which the infinity space is alone present. And passing out of the mere consciousness of the infinity of space he entered into the fourth stage of deep meditation. And passing out of the fourth stage he entered into the third. And passing out of the third stage he entered into the second. And passing out of the second he entered into the first. And passing out of the first stage of deep meditation he entered into the second. And passing out of the second stage he enetered into the third. And passing out of the third stage he entered into the fourth stage of deep meditation. And passing out of the last stage of deep meditation he immediately expired.

Earthquake...

When the Blessed One died there arose, at the moment of his passing out of existence, a mighty earthquake, terrible and awe-inspiring; and the thunders of heaven burst forth.

When the Blessed One died, Brahma Sahampati, at the moment of his passing away from existence, uttered this stanza:

'They all, all beings that have life, shall lay
Aside their complex form—that aggregation
Of mental and material qualities,
That gives them, or in heaven or on earth,
Their fleeting individuality!
E'en as the teacher—being such a one,
Unequalled among all the men that are,
Successor of the prophets of old time,
Mighty by wisdom, and in insight clear—
Hath died!'

When the Blessaed One died, Sakka, the king of the gods, at the moment of his passing away from existence, uttered this stanza:

'They're transient all, each being's parts and powers,
Growth is their nature, and decay.
They are produced, they are dissolved again:
And then is best, when they have sunk to rest!'

When the Blessed One died, the venerable Anuruddha, at the moment of his passing away from existence, uttered these stanzas:

'When he who from all craving want was free,
Who to Nirvana's tranquil state had reached,
When the great sage finished his span of life,
Now gasping struggle vexed that steadfast heart!
All resolute, and with unshaken mind,
He calmly triumphed o'er the pain of death.
E'en as a bright flame dies away, so was
His last deliverance from the bonds of life!'

When the Blessed One died, the venerable Ananda, at the moment of his passing away from existence, uttered this stanza:

'Then was there terror!
Then stood the hair on end
When he endowed with every grace—
The supreme Buddha—died!'

When the Blessed One died, of those of the brethren who were not yet free from the passions, some stretched out their arms and wept, and some fell headlong on the ground, rolling to and fro in anguish at the thought: 'Too soon has the Blessed One died! Too soon has the Happy One passed away from existence! Too soon has the Light gone out in the world!'

But those of the brethren who were free from the passions 'the Arahats' bore their grief collected and composed at the thought: 'Impermanent are all component things! How is it possible that they should not be dissolved?'

'Weep not, neither lament...'

Then the venerable Anuruddha exhorted the brethren, and said: 'Enough, my brethren! Weep not, neither lament!

Has not the Blessed One formerly declared this to us, that it is in the very nature of all things near and dear unto us, that we must divide ourselves from them, leave them, sever ourselves from them? How then, brethren, can this be possible—that whereas anything whatever born, brought into being, and organised, contains within itself the inherent necessity of dissolution—how then can this be possible that such a being should not be dissolved? No such condition can exist! Even the spirits, brethren, will reproach us.'

'But of what kind of spirits is the Lord, the venerable Anuruddha, thinking?'

'There are spirits, brother Ananda, in the sky but of worldly mind, who dishevel their hair and weep, and stretch forth their arms and weep, fall prostrate on the ground, and roll to and fro in anguish at the thought: "Too soon has the Blessed One died! Too soon has the Happy One passed away! Too soon has the Light gone out in the world!'

'There are spiritis, too, Ananda, on the earth, and of worldly mind, who tear their hair, and weep, and stretch forth their arms and weep, fall prostrate on the ground, and roll to and fro in anguish at the thought: "Too soon has the Blessed One died! Too soon has the Happy One passed away! Too soon has the Light gone out in the world!"

'But the spirits who are free from passion bear it, calm and self-possessed, mindful of the saying which begins, "Impermanent indeed are all component things. How then is it possible that such a being should not be dissolved?'

Afterward...

Now the venerable Anuruddha and the venerable Ananda spent the rest of that night in religious discourse. Then the venerable Anuruddha said to the venerable Ananda: 'Go now, brother Ananda, into Kusinara and inform the Mallas of Kusinara, saying, 'The Blessed One, O Vasetthas, is dead; do, then, whatever seems to you fit!'

'Even so, Lord!' said the venerable Ananda, in assent, to the venerable Anuruddha. And having robed himself early in the morning, he took his bowl, and went into Kusinara with one of the brethren as an attendant.

Now at that time the Mallas of Kusinara were assembled in the council hall concerning that very matter.

And the venerable Ananda went to the council hall of the Mallas of Kusinara; and when he had arrived there, he informed them, saying, 'The Blessed One, O Vasetthas, is dead; do, then, whatever seemes to you fit!'

And when they had heard this saying of the venerable Ananda, the Mallas, with their young men and their maidens and their wives, were grieved, and sad, and afflicted at heart. And some of them wept, dishevelling their hair, and some stretched forth their arms and wept, and some fell prostrate on the ground, and some reeled to and fro in anguish at the thought: 'Too soon has the Blessed One died! Too soon has the Happy One passed away! Too soon has the Light gone out in the world!'

Then the Mallas of Kusinara gave orders to their attendants, saying, 'Gather together perfumes and garlands, and all the music in Kusinara!'

And the Mallas of Kusinara took the perfumes and garlands, and all the musical instruments, and five hundred suits of apparel, and went to the Upavattana, to the Sala Grove of the Mallas, where the body of the Blessed One lay. There they past the day in paying honour, reverence, respect, and homage to the remains of the Blessed One with dancing, and hymns, and music, and with garlands and perfumes; and in making canopies of their garments, and preparing decoration wreaths to hang thereon.

Then the Mallas of Kusinara thought:

'It is much too late to burn the body of the Blessed One to-day. Let us now perform the cremation tomorrow.' And

Light gone out!

in paying honour, reverence, respect, and homage to the remains of the Blessed One with dancing, and hymns and music, and with garlands and perfumes; and in making canopies of their garments, and preparing decoration wreaths to hang thereon, they past the second day, too, and then the third day, and the fourth, and the fifth, and the sixth day also.

Then on the seventh day the Mallas of Kusinara thought:

'Let us carry the body of the Blessed One, by the south and outside, to a spot on the south, and outside of the city—paying it honour, and reverence, and respect, and homage, with dance and song and music, and homage, with garlands and perfumes—and there, to the south of the city, let us perform the cremation ceremony!'

And thereupon eight chieftains among the Mallas bathed their heads, and clad themselves in new garments with the intention of bearing the body of the Blessed One. But, behold, they could not lift it up!

Then the Mallas of Kusinara said to the venerable Anuruddha: 'What, Lord, can be the reason, what can be the cause that eight chieftains of the Mallas who have bathed their heads, and clad themselves in new garments with the intention of bearing the body of the Blessed One, are unable to lift it up?'

'It is because you, O Vasetthas, have one purpose, and the spirits have another purpose.'

'But what, Lord, is the purpose of the spirits?:

'Your purpose, O Vasetthas, is this, Let us carry the body of the Blessed One, by the south and outside, to a spot on the south, and outside of the city,—paying it honour, and reverence, and respect, and homage, with dance and song and music, with garlands, and perfumes—and there, to the south of the city, let us perform the cremation ceremony. But the purpose of the spirits, Vasetthas, is this: Let us carry the body of the Blessed

One by the north to the north of the city, and entering the city by the north gate, let us bring it through the midst of the city into the midst thereof. And going out again by the eastern gate—paying honour, and reverence, and respect, and homage to the body of the Blessed One, with heavenly dance, and song, and music, and garlands, and perfumes—let us carry it to the shrine of the Mallas called Makuta-bandhana, to the east of the city; and there let us perform the cremation ceremony.'

'Even according to the purpose of the spirits, so, Lord, let it be!'

Then immediately all Kusinara down even to the dust bins and rubbish heaps became strewn knee-deep with Mandarava flowers from heaven! and while both the spirits from the skies, and the Mallas of Kusinara upon earth, paid honour, and reverence, and respect, and homage to the body of the Blessed One, with perfumes, they carried the body by the north to the north of the city; and entering the city by the gate they carried it through the midst of the city into the midst thereof; and going out again by the eastern gate they carried it to the shrine of the Mallas, called Makuta-bandhana; and there, to the east of the city, they laid down the body of the Blessed One.

Then the Mallas of Kusinara said to the venerable Ananda: 'What should be done, Lord, with the remains of the Tathagata?'

'As men treat the remains of a king of kings, so, Vasetthas, should they treat the remains of the Tathagata.'

'And how, Lord, do they treat the remains of a king of kings?'

'They wrap the body of a king of kings, Vasetthas, in a new cloth. When that is done they wrap it in cotton wool. When that is done, they wrap it in a new cloth,—and so on till they have wrapped the body in five hundred successive layers of both kinds. Then they place the body in an oil vssel of iron, and cover that close up with another oil vessel of iron. They then build a funeral pile of all kinds of perfumes, and burn the body of the king of kings. And then at the four cross-roads they erect a dagaba to the king of kings. This, Vasetthas, is the way in which they treat the remains of a king of kings.

'And as they treat the remains of a king of kings, so, Vasetthas, should they treat the remains of the Tathagata. At the four cross-roads a dagaba should be erected to the Tathagata. And whosoever shall there place garlands or perfumes or paint, or make salutation there, or become in its presence calm in heart—that shall long be to them for a profit and a joy.'

Therefore the Mallas gave orders to their attendants, saying, 'Gather together all the carded cotton wool of the Mallas!'

Then the Mallas of Kusinara wrapped the body of the Blessed One in a new cloth. And when that was done, they wrapped it in cotton wool. And when that was done, they wrapped it in a new cloth,—and so on till they had wrapped the body of the Blessed One in five hundred layers of both kinds. And then they placed the body in an oil vessel of iron, and covered that close up with another oil vessel of iron. And then they built a funeral pile of all kinds of perfumes, and upon it they placed the body of the Blessed One.

Now at that time the venerable Maha Kassapa was journeying along the high road from Pava to Kusinara with a great company of the brethren, with about five hundred of the brethren. And the venerable Maha Kassapa left the high road, and sat himself down at the foot of a certain tree.

Just at that time a certain naked ascetic who had picked up a Mandarava flower in Kusinara was coming along the high road to Pava.

And the venerable Maha Kassapa saw the naked ascetic coming in the distance; and when he had seen him he said to the naked ascetic:

'O friend! surely thou knowest our Master?'

'Yes, friend! I know him. This day the Samana Gotama has been dead a week! That is how I obtained this Mandarava flower.'

And immediately of those of the brethren who were not yet free from the passions, some stretched out their arms and wept, and some fell headlong on the ground, and some reeled to and fro in anguish at the thought: 'Too soon has the Blessed One died! Too soon has the Happy One passed away from existence! Too soon has the Light gone out in the world!'

But those of the brethren who were free from the passions, the Arahats bore their grief collected and composed at the thought: 'Impermanent are all component things! How is it possible that they should not be dissolved?'

Now at that time a brother named Subhadda, who had been received into the order in his old age, was seated there in their company.

And Subhadda the old addressed the brethren, and said: 'Enough, brethren! Weep not, neither lament! We are well rid of the great Samana. We used to be annoyed by being told, "This beseems you, this beseems you not." But now we shall be able to do whatever we like; and what we do not like, that we shall not have to do!'

But the venerable Maha Kassapa addressed the brethren, and said: 'Enough, my brethren! Weep not, neither lament! Has not the Blessed One formerly declared this to us, that it is in the very nature of all things, near and dear unto us, that we must divide ourselves from them, leave them, sever ourselves from them? How then, brethren, can this be possible—that whereas anything whatever born, brought itself the inherent necessity of dissolution—how then can this be possible that such a being should not be dissolved? No such condition can exist!'

The funeral

Now just at that time four chieftains of the Mallas had bathed their heads and clad themselves in new garments with the intention of setting on fire the funeral pile of the Blessed One. But, behold, they were unable to set it alight!

Then the Mallas of Kusinara said to the venerable Anuruddha: 'What, Lord, can be the reason, and what the cause, that four chieftains of the Mallas who have bathed their heads and clad themselves in new garments, with the intention of setting on fire the funeral pile of the Blessed One, are unable to set it on fire?'

'It is because you, O Vasetthas, have one purpose, and the spirits have another purpose.'

'But what, Lord, is the purpose of the spirits?'

'The purpose of the spirits, O Vasetthas, is this: That venerable brother Maha Kassapa is now journeying along the high road from Pava to Kussinara with a great company of the brethren, with five hundred of the brethren. The funeral pile of the Blessed One shall not catch fire, until the venerable Maha Kassapa shall have been able reverently to salute the sacred feet of the Blessed One.'

'Even according to the purpose of the spirits, so, Lord, let it be!'

Then the venerable Maha Kassapa went to Makuta-bandhana of Kusinara to the shrine of the Mallas, to the place where the funeral pile of the Blessed One was. And when he had come up to it, he arranged his robe on one shoulder; and bowing down with clasped hands, he thrice walked reverently round the pile; and then, uncovering the feet, he bowed down in reverence at the feet of the Blessed One.

And those five hundred brethern arranged their robes on one shoulder; and bowing down with clasped hands, they thrice walked reverently round the pile, and then bowed down in reverence at the feet of the Blessed One.

LORD BUDDHA'S BONE RELICS

Discovered in the ruins of Kanishka's stupa at Peshawar. The casket is of dark metal and is seven inches high. Contained a rock-crystal reliquary containing bones, said to be Buddha's. On top of the casket Buddha and two other figures. Note the haloes. Beneath is Kanishka himself.

And when the homage of the venerable Maha Kassapa and of those five hundred brethren was ended, the funeral pile of the Blessed One caught fire of itself.

Now as the body of the Blessed One burned itself away, from the skin and the integument, and the flesh, and the nerves, and the fluid of the joints, neither soot nor ash was seen; and only the bones remained behind.

Just as one sees no soot or ash when glue or oil is burned; so, as the body of the Blessed One burned itself away, from the skin and the integument, and the flesh, and the nerves, and the fluid of the joints, neither soot nor ash was seen; and only the bones remained behind. And of those five hundred pieces of raiment the very innermost and outermost were both consumed.

And when the body of the Blessed One had been burnt up, there came down streams of water from the sky and extinguished the funeral pile of the Blessed One; and there burst forth streams of water from the storehouse of the waters beneath the earth, and extinguished the funeral pile of the Blessed One. The Mallas of Kusinara also brought water scented with all kinds of perfumes and extinguished the funeral pile of the Blessed One.

Then the Mallas of Kusinara surrounded the bones of the Blessed One in their council hall with a lattice work of spears and with a rampart of bows; and there for seven days they paid honour and reverence and respect and homage to them with dance and song and music, and with garlands and perfumes.

The relics

Now the king of Magadha, Ajatasattu, the son of the queen of the Videha clan, heard the news that the Blessed One had died at Kusinara.

Then the king of Magadha, Ajatasattu, the son of the queen of the Videha clan, sent a messenger to the Mallas, saying, 'The Blessed One belonged to the soldier caste, and I too am of the soldier caste. I am worthy to receive a portion of the relics of the Blessed One. Over the remains of the Blessed One will I put up a sacred cairn, and in their honour will I celebrate a feast.'

And the Lichchhavis of Vesali heard the news that the Blessed One had died at Kusinara. And the Lichchhavis of Vesali sent a messenger to the Mallas, saying, 'The Blessed One belonged to the soldier caste, and we too are of the soldier caste. We are worthy to receive a portion of the relics of the Blessed One. Over the remains of the Blessed One will we put up a sacred cairn, and in their honour will we celebrate a feast.

And the Sakiyas of Kapilavatthu heard the news that the Blessed One had died at Kusinara. And the Sakiyas of Kapilavatthu sent a messenger to the Mallas, saying, 'The Blessed One was the pride of our race. We are worthy to receive a portion of the relics of the Blessed One. Over the remains of the Blessed One will we put up a sacred cairn, and in their honour will we celebrate a feast!'

And the Bulis of Allakappa heard the news that the Blessed One had died at Kusinara. And the Bulis of Allakappa sent a messenger to the Mallas saying, 'The Blessed One belonged to the soldier caste, and we too are of the soldier caste. We are worthy to receive a portion of the relics of the Blessed One. Over the remains of the Blessed One will we put up a sacred cairn, and in their honour will we celebrate a feast!'

And the Koliyas of Ramagama heard the news that the Blessed One had died at Kusinara. And the Koliyas of Ramagama sent a messenger to the Mallas saying, 'The Blessed One belonged to the soldier caste, and we too are of the soldier caste. We are worthy to receive a portion of the relics of the Blessed One. Over the remains of the Blessed One will we put up a sacred cairn, and in their honour will we celebrate a feast!'

And the Brahmin of Vethadipa heard the news that the Blessed One had died at Kusinara. And the Brahmin of

Vethadipa sent a messenger to the Mallas, saying, 'The Blessed One belonged to the soldier caste, and I am a Brahmin. I am worthy to receive a portion of the Blessed One. Over the remains of the Blessed One will I put up a sacred cairn, and in their honour will I celebrate a feast!'

And the Mallas of Pava heard the news that the Blessed One had died at Kusinara.

Then the Mallas of Pava sent a messenger to the Mallas saying, 'The Blessed One belonged to the soldier caste, and we too are of the soldier caste. We are worthy to receive a portion of the relics of the Blessed One. Over the remains of the Blessed One will we put up a sacred cairn, and in their honour will we celebrate a feast!'

When they heard these things the Mallas of Kusinara spoke to the assembled brethren, saying, 'The Blessed One died in our village domain. We will not give away any part of the remains of the Blessed One!'

When they had thus spoken, Dona the Brahmin addressed the assembled brethren, and said :

'Hear, revered sirs, one single word from me.
Forbearance was our Buddha want to teach.
Unseemly is it that over the division
Of the remains of him who was the best of beings
Strife should arise, and wounds, and war!
Let us all, sirs, with one accord unite
In friendly harmony to make eight portions.
Wide spread let Thupas rise in every land
That in the Enlightened One mankind may trust!'

'Do thou then, O Brahmin, thyself divide the remains of the Blessed One equally into eight parts, with fair division.'

'Be it so, sir!' said Dona, in assent, to the assembled brethren. And he divided the remains of the Blessed One equally into eight parts, with fair divisions. And he said to them: 'Give me, sirs, this vessel, and I will set up over it a sacred cairn, and in its honour will I establish a feast.'

And they gave the vessel to Dona the Brahmin.

And the Moriyas of Pipphalivana heard the news that the Blessed One had died at Kusinara.

Then the Moriyas of Pipphalivana sent a messenger to the Mallas, saying, 'The Blessed One belonged to the soldier caste, and we too are of the soldier caste. We are worthy to receive a portion of the relics of the Blessed One. Over the remains of the Blessed One will we put up a sacred cairn and in their honour will we celebrate a feast!'

And when they heard the answer, saying, 'There is no portion of the remains of the Blessed One left over. The remains of the Blessed One are all distributed,' then they took away the embers.

Then the king of Magadha, Ajatasattu, son of the queen of the Videha clan, made a mound in Rajagaha over the remains of the Blessed One, and held a feast.

And the Lichihhavis of Vesali made a mound in Vesali over the remains of the Blessed One, and held a feast.

And the Bulis of Allakappa made a mound in Allakappa over the remains of the Blessed One, and held a feast.

And the Koliyas of Ramagama made a mound in Ramagama over the remains of the Blessed One, and held a feast.

And Vethadipaka the Brahmin made a mound in Vethadipa over the remains of the Blessed One, and held a feast.

And the Mallas of Pava made a mound in Pava over the remains of the Blessed One, and held a feast.

And the Mallas of Kusinara made a mound in Kusinara over the remains of the Blessed One, and held a feast.

And Dona the Brahmin made a mound over the vessel in which the body had been burnt, and held a feast.

And the Moriyas of Pipphalivana made a mound over the embers, and held a feast.

Thus were there eight mound Thupas for the remains, and one for the vessel, and one for the embers. This was how it used to be.

Eight measures of relics there were of him of the far-seeing eye,
Of the best of the best of men. In India seven are worshipped.
And one measure in Ramagama, by the kings of the serpent race.
One tooth, too, is honoured in heaven and one in Gandhara's city,
One in the Kalinga realm, and one more by the Naga race.
Through their glory the bountiful earth is made bright with offerings painless—
For with such are the Great Teacher's relics best honoured by those who are honoured,
By gods and by Nagas and kings, yea, thus by the noblest of monarchs—
Bow down with clasped hands!
Hard, hard is a Buddha to meet with through
Hundreds of ages!

The last sleep!

In Pure Land

THE LAND OF BLISS

Sukhavati Vyuha

Translated by

F. Max Muller

Lord Buddha, Java

The Sutra

ACCORDING to the census of 1891, Japan has about forty millions of inhabitants, of whom more than thirty millions are Buddhists. Of these Buddhists the Shin-shiu sect claims about ten millions of followers, with 19,208 temples, and 11,958 preachers, with ten chief priests, and 3,593 students. The books on which the members of this sect chiefly found their faith are the two Sukhavati Vyuhas, the large and the small, and the Amitayur-dhyana Sutra. They are sometimes called the Large Sutra, the Small Sutra and the Sutra of Meditation.

According to the Buddhists of Japan, Buddha preached the Amitayur-dhyana Sutra to queen Vaidehi in the city of Rajagriha. This was during the fifth period of his life; when he was between the age of seventy-one and seventy-nine.

Vaidehi, consort of king Bimbisara of Magadha, seeing the wicked actions of her son Ajatasatru, began to feel weary of this world. Sakyamuni then taught her how to be born in the Pure Land Sukhavati, instructing her in the method of being born in that world, enumerating three kinds of good actions. The first is worldly goodness, which includes good actions in general, such as filial piety, respect for elders, loyalty, faithfulness, etc. The second is the goodness of Sila or morality, all who do not oppose the general rule of reproving wickedness and exhorting to the practice of virtue, are included in this goodness: The third is the goodness of practice, which includes that of the four Satyas or truths, and the six Paramitas or perfections. Towards the end of the Sutra, Buddha says: "Let not one's voice cease, but ten times complete the thought, and repeat the words 'Namo-mitabhaya Buddhaya,' or Adoration to

Amitabha Buddha. This practice is the most excellent of all."

The same three books, that is, the two Sukhavati Vyuhas and the Amitayur-dhyana Sutra, form also the chief authority of the Jodoshiu sect of the Pure Land.

Chinese translations of these texts were known to exist not only in China, but also in Japan, and in several cases more than one translation of the same text.

The Larger and the Smaller Sukhavati Vyuha differ from each other on several smaller points. The Larger Sukhvati vyuha is represented as having been preached on the Gridhrrkuta hill near Rajagriha, the Smaller Sukhvati Vyuha in the Jeta-grove near Sravasti. In the former the chief interlocutors are the Bhagvat, i.e., the Buddha Sakyamuni, Ananda and Ajita; in the latter the Bhagvat and Sariputra.

There is one point, however, which is of great importance in the eyes of the followers of the Shin-shiu sect, on which the two treatises differ.

The Smaller Sukhvati Vyuha lays great stress on the fact that people can be saved or can be born in the Land of Bliss, if only they remember and repeat the name of Buddha Amitabha two, three, four, five, six or more nights before their death, and it distinctly denies that people are born in the Paradise of Amitabha as a reward or necessary result of good works performed in the present life. This would seem to take away one of the fundamental doctrines of Buddhism, namely, the doctrine of Karman, or of the continuous working of our deeds whether good or bad. Instead of the old doctrine, as a man soweth, so he shall reap. A new and easier way of salvation is here preached. As a man prayeth, so he shall be saved.'It is what is known to us as salvation by faith rather than by works. The Larger Sukhvati Vyuha lays great stress on prayer and faith in Amitabha, but it never neglects 'the stock of merit' as essential for salvation. It would almost seem as if this popular and easy doctrine had secured to itself the name of Mahayana, as meaning the Broad Way, in opposition to the Narrow Way, the Hinayana.

Even in our Sukhavati Vyuha the teacher, the Bhagvat is Sakyamuni. We begin with a dialogue between this Buddha and his famous disciple Ananda. Ananda asks him what he is seeing or thinking. Thereupon Buddha relates how there was a line of eighty-one Tathagatas or Buddhas beginning with Dipankara and ending with Lokeswararaja. During the period of this Tathagata Lokesvararaja, a Bhikshu or Buddhist mendicant of the name of Dharmakara formed the intention of becoming a Buddha. He therefore went to the Tathagata Lokesvararaja, praised him in several verses, and then asked him to become his teacher. After having received instruction, Dharmakara comprehended all the best qualities of all the Buddha countries, and prayed that they should all be concentrated in his own country when he himself had become a Buddha.

After long meditations Dharmakara returns to Buddha Lokesvararaja and tells him in a long prayer what he wishes and wills his own Buddha country to be. This prayer forms the nucleus of the Sukhavati Vyuha; it is a kind of prophecy of what, according to Dharmakara's ideas, Sukhavati or what, according to Dharmakara's ideas, Sukhavati or the Land of Bliss ought to be. Dharmakara then became a Bodhisattva, a candidate for Buddhahood, and lastly, a real Buddha. When Ananda asks Sakyamuni what has become of this Bodhisattva Dharmakara, Buddha answers that this original mendicant is now reigning in Sukhavati as the Buddha Amitabha.

He then proceeds to describe Sukhavati where Amitabha dwells. Once Ananda is reproved by Buddha for not implicitly believing all he says about the marvels of Sukhavati, but afterwards the praises of Sukhavati and of its inhabitants are continued till nearly the end. At last Ananda expresses a wish to see Amitabha, whereupon that Buddha sends a ray of .light from the palm of his hand so that the whole world was inundated by its light, and not only Ananda, but every living being could see Amitabha and his retinue of Bodhisattvas in the Land of Bliss, while they in Sukhavati could see Sakyamuni and the whole world.

Then begins the conversation between Sakyamuni and Ajita instead of Ananda. Buddha explains to him how some of the blessed spirits in Sukhavati sit cross-legged in lotus-flowers, while others dwell shut up in the calyx of these flowers, the former being the firm believers in Amitabha, the latter those who have entertained some doubt, and who have therefore to wait for five hundred years inside the calyx before they become full-blown. In conclusion Buddha Sakyamuni exhorts Ajita to teach this treatise, the Sukhavati Vyuha, to all beings, and promises great rewards to all who learn it, copy it, teach and explain it.

I hardly thought then that Mahayana texts like the Sukhavati Vyuha, which seemed to be of so secondary a character, would claim a foremost place. The first Chinese translation of it by Lokaraksha was made between the years 147-186 A.D.; the second by K'Khien between 223-253 A.D.; and the third and best by Sanghavarman, an Indian sramana of Tibetan origin, in 252 A.D. The doctrine of Amitabha and his paradise Sukhavati seems to have acquired great popularity in China and after easy salvation was made by it.

The Buddhists who, as I have pointed out on several occasions, are the debtors of the Brahmins in almost all their philosophical speculations, seem to me to have borrowed also their half-mythological conception of Sukhavati or the Land of Bliss from the same source. In the Vishnu and other Puranas, when the cities of the Lokapala gods are mentioned, in the different quarters of the sky, the city of Varuna is placed in the West, and it is called Mukhya, the chief, or Sukha, the happy, or Nimochani, the city of sunset. This Sukha is, I think, the prototype of Sukhavati.

In Japan, where Buddhism was introduced by way of Korea in 552 A.D., when the emperor Jomei held a religious service at his palace to hear an exposition of the Sutra on Sukhavati from the lips of Ye-yin, a sramana invited from China. Many works were composed in Japan as well as in China on Amitabha and his Paradise.

—F. Max Muller

Oxford: Jan. 26, 1894

Apsaras

The Land of Bliss

OM. Adoration to the Three Treasures! Om. Adoration to all the glorious Buddhas and Bodhisattvas! Adoration to all Buddhas, Bodhisattvas, Aryas, Sravakas, and Pratyekabuddhas, past, present, and to come, who dwell in the unlimited and endless Lokadhatus of the ten quarters! Adoration to Amitabha! Adoration to him whose soul is endowed with incomprehensible virtues!

Adoration to Amitabha, to the Jina, to thee, O Muni!

I go to Sukhavati through thy compassion also; To Sukhavati, with its groves, resplendent with gold, The delightful, adorned with the sons of Sugata, —I go to it, which is full of many jewels and treasures; And the refuge of thee, the famous and wise.

Thus it was heard by me:

At one time the Bhagavat dwelt in Rajagriha, on the mountain Gridhrakuta, with a large assembly of Bhikshus, with thirty-two thousand of Bhikshus, all holy (arhat), free from frailties and cares, who had performed their religious duties, whose thoughts had been thoroughly freed through perfect knowledge, with inquiring thoughts, who had broken the fetters of existence, who had obtained their desires, who had conquered, who had achieved the highest self-restraint, whose thoughts and whose knowledge were unfettered, Mahanagas (great heroes), possessed of the six kinds of knowledge, self-controlled, meditating on the eight kinds of salvation, possessed of the powers, wise in wisdom, elders, great disciples, 1. Ajnatakaundinya, 2. Asvajit, 3. Vashpa, 4. Mahanaman, 5. Bhadrajit, 6. Yasodeva, 7. Vimala, 8. Subahu, 9. Purna Maitrayaniputra,

10. Uruvilva-kasyapa, 11. Nadi-kasyapa, 12. Gaya-kasyapa, 13. Kumara-kasyapa, 14. Maha-kasyapa, 15. Sariputra, 16. Mahamaudgalyayana, 17. Mahakaushthilya, 18. Mahakapila, 19. Mahachunda, 20. Aniruddha, 21. Nandika, 22. Kampila, 23. Subhuti, 24. Revata, 25. Khadiravanika, 26. Vakula, 27. Svagata, 28. Amogharaja, 29. Parayanika, 30. Patka, 31. Chullapatka, 32. Nanda, 33. Rahula, and 34. the blessed Ananda,—with these and with other elders, and great disciples, who were wise in wisdom, with the exception of one person who had still to be advanced on the path of the disciples, the blessed Ananda;—and with many noble-minded Bodhisattvas, led by Maitreya.

Then the blessed Ananda, having risen from his seat, having put his cloak on one shoulder, and knelt on the earth with his right knee, making obeisance with folded hands in the direction of the Bhagavat, spoke thus to the Bhagavat: 'Thy organs of sense, O Bhagavat, are serene, the colour of thy skin is clear, the colour of thy face bright and yellowish. As an autumn cloud is pale, clear, bright and yellowish, thus the organs of sense of the Bhagavat are serene, the colour of his face is clear, the colour of his skin bright and yellowish. And as, O Bhagavat, a piece of gold coming from the Jambu river, having been thrown into a furnace by a clever smith or by his apprentice, and well fashioned, when thrown on a pale cloth, looks extremely clear, bright and yellowish, thus the organs of sense of the Bhagavat are serene, the colour of his face is clear, and the colour of his skin bright and yellowish. Moreover, I do not know, O Bhagavat, that I have ever seen the organs of sense of the Tathagata so serene, the colour of his face so clear, and the colour of his skin so bright and yellowish before now. This thought occurs to me, O Bhagavat: probably, the Tathagata dwells today in the state of a Buddha, probably the Tathagata dwells today in the state of Jina, in the state of omniscience, in the state of a Mahanaga; and he contemplates the holy and fully enlightened Tathagatas of the past, future, and present.'

After these words, the Bhagavat thus spoke to the blessed Ananda: 'Well said! well said! Ananda. Did the gods suggest this matter to you? or the blessed Buddhas? Or.do you know this through the philosophical knowledge which you possess?'

After these words the blessed Ananda spoke thus to the Bhagavat: 'The gods, O Bhagavat, do not suggest this matter to me, nor the blessed Buddhas, but this thought occurs to me by my own philosophy alone, that probably the Tathagata dwells today in the state of a Buddha, probably the Tathagata dwells today in the state of Jina, in the state of omniscience, in the state of a Mahanaga; or he contemplates the venerable Buddha of the past, future, and present.'

After these words the Bhagavat spoke thus to the blessed Ananda: 'Well said! well said! Ananda; excellent indeed is your question.;—good your philosophy, and beautiful your understanding! You, O Ananda, have arrived for the benefit and happiness of many people, out of compassion for the world, for the sake of the great body of men, for the benefit and happiness of gods and men, as you think it right to ask the Tathagata this matter: Thus, indeed, Ananda might pile up intellectual knowledge under immeasurable and innumerable blessed, holy, and fully enlightened Tathagatas and yet the knowledge of the Tathagata would not be exceeded thereby. And why? Because, O Ananda, one who possesses the knowledge of a Tathagata possesses an intellectual knowledge of causes that cannot be exceeded. If the Tathagata wished, O Ananda, he could live for a whole kalpa on one alms-gift, or for a hundred kalpas, or for a thousand kalpas, or for a hundred thousand kalpas, to a hundred thousand niyutas of kotis of kalpas, nay, he could live beyond, and yet the organs of nature of the Tathagata would not perish, the colour of his face would not be altered, nor would the colour of his skin be injured. And why? Because, O Ananda, the Tathagata has so fully obtained the Paramitas which arise from Samadhi. The appearance of fully enlightened Buddhas is very difficult to be obtained in this world, O

Ananda. As the appearance of Audumbara flowers is very difficult to be obtained in this world; thus, O Ananda, the appearance of Tathagatas who desire welfare, wish for what is beneficial, are compassionate, and have arrived at the highest compassion, is very difficult to be obtained. But, O Ananda, it is owing to the grace of the Tathagata himself that you think that the Tathagata should be asked this question, so that there may arise in this world beings who can be teachers of all the world, for the sake of noble-minded Bodhisattvas. Therefore, O Ananda, listen, and take it well and rightly to heart! I shall tell you.'

'Yes, O Bhagavat,' so did the blessed Ananda answer the Bhagavat.

The Bhagavat then spoke to Ananda: 'At the time, O Ananda, which was long ago in the past, in an innumerable and more than innumerable, enormous, immeasurable, and incomprehensible kalpa before now, —at that time, and at that moment, there arose in the world a holy and fully enlightened Tathagata called 1. Dipankara. Following after Dipankara, O Ananda, there was a Tathagata 2. Pratapavat, and after him, 3. Prabhakara, 4. Chandanagandha, 5. Sumerukalpa, 6. Chandana, 7. Vimalajnana, 8. Anupalipta, 9. Vimalaprabha, 10. Nagabhibhu, 11. Suryodana, 12. Girirajaghosha, 13. Merukuta, 14. Suvarnaprabha, 15.Jyotishprabha, 16. Vaiduryanir-bhasa, 17. Brahmaghosha, 18. Chandabhibhu, 19. Turyaghosha, 20. Muktakusumapratimanitaprabha, 21. Srikuta, 22. Sagaravarabuddhivikriditabhijna, 23. Varaprabha, 24. Mahagandharanirbhasa, 25. Vyapagatakhilamalapratighosha, 26. Surakta, 27. Rananjaya, 28. Mahagunadharabuddhipraptabhijna, 29. Chandrasu-ryajihmikarana, 30. Uttaptavaidu-ryanirbhasa, 31. Chittadharabuddhisankusumitabhyudgata, 32. Pushpavativanarajasankusumitabhija, 33. Pushpakara, 34. Udakachandra 35. Avidyandhakaravidhvamsanakara, 36. Lokendra, 37. Muktachchhatrapravatasadrisa, 38. Tishya, 39. Dharmamativinanditaraja, 40. Simhasagarakutavinanditaraja, 41. Sagarameruchandra, 42. Brahmasvaranadabhinandita, 43. Kusumasambhava, 44. Praptasena, 45. Chandra bhanu, 46. Merukuta, 47. Chandraprabha, 48. Vim-alanetra, 49. Girirajaghoshesvara, 50. Kusumaprabha, 51. Kusumavrishtyabhiprakirna, 52. Ratnachandra, 53. Padmabimbyupasobhita, 54. Chandanagandha, 55. Ratnabhibhasa, 56. Nimi, 57. Mahavyuha, 58. Vyapagatakhiladosha, 59. Brahmaghosha, 60. Saptaratnabhivrishta, 61. Mahajunadhara, 62. Mahatamalapatrachandanakardama, 63. Kusumabhijna, 64. Ajnanavidhvamsana, 65. Kesarin, 66.Muktachchhatra, 67. Suvarnagarbha, 68. Vaiduryagarbha, 69. Mahaketu, 70. Dharmaketu, 71. Ratnaketu, 72. Ratnasri, 73. Lokendra, 74. Narendra, 75. Karunika, 76. Lokasundara, 77. Brahmaketu, 78. Dharmamati, 79. Simha, 80. Simhamati.

After Simhamati, a holy and fully enlightened Tathagata arose in the world, Lokesvararaja by name, perfect in knowledge and conduct, a Sugata, knowing the world, without a superior, charioteer of men whose passions have to be tamed, teacher of gods and men, a Buddha, a Bhagavat. And again during the time of the preaching of this holy and fully enlightened Tathagata Lokesvararaja, O Ananda, there was a Bhikshu, Dharmakara by name, richly endowed with memory, with understanding, prudence, and wisdom, richly endowed with vigour, and of noble character.

'Then, O Ananda, that Bhikshu Dharmakara, having risen from his seat, having put his cloak on one shoulder, and knelt on the earth with his right knee, stretching forth his folded hands to where the Bhagavat Tathagata Lokesvararaja was, and, after worshipping the Bhagavat, he, at that very time, praised him in his presence with these Gathas:

" O thou of immeasurabie light, whose knowledge is endless and incomparable; not any other light can shine herewhere thou art! The rays of the moon of Siva and of the jewel of the sun, were not bright here in the whole world.

"The form also is infinite in the best of beings; thus also the voice of Buddha is of infinite sound; his virtue likewise, with meditation, knowledge strength; like unto thee there is no one in this world.

"The Law (dharma) is deep, wide, and subtle; the best of Buddhas is incomprehensible, like the ocean; therefore there is no further exaltation of the teacher; having left all faults, he is gone to the other shore.

"Then the best of Buddhas, of endless light, lights up all regions, he the king of kings; and I, having become Buddha, and a master of the Law, may I deliver mankind from old age and death.

"And I, on the strength of generosity, equanimity, virtue, forbearance, power, meditation and absorption, undertake here the first and best duties, and shall become a Buddha, the saviour of all beings.

"And I, seeking for the knowledge of the best of the Blessed Ones, shall always worship many hundred thousands of kotis of Buddhas, endless like the sand of the Ganga, the incomparable lords.

"Whatever worlds there are, similar in number to the sand of the Ganga, and the endless countries which exist besides, there everywhere I shall send out light, because I have attained such power.

"My land is to be noble, the first and the best; the Bodhi-tree excellent in this world. There is incomparable happiness arising from Nirvana, and this also I shall explain as vain.

"Beings come hither from the ten quarters; having arrived here they quickly show me happiness. May Buddha there teach me the truth, —I form a desire full of true strength and vigour.

"I, knowing the worlds of the ten quarters, possessed of absolute knowledge—they also always proclaim my thought! May I, gone to Avichi hell, always abide there, but I shall never cease to practise the power of prayer! [i.e., May I remain in hell, if I cease to pray.]"

'Then, O Ananda, that Bhikshu Dharmakara, having praised the Bhagavat, the Tathagata Lokesvararaja, in his presence, with those Gathas, spoke thus: "O Bhagavat, I wish to know the highest perfect knowledge. Again and again I raise and incline my thoughts towards the highest perfect knowledge. May therefore the Bhagavat, as a teacher, thus teach me the Law, that I may quickly know the highest perfect knowledge. May I become in the world a Tathagata, equal to the unequalled. And may the Bhagavat proclaim those signs by which I may comprehend the perfection of all good qualities of a Buddha country."

'After this, O Ananda, the Bhagavat Lokesvararaja, the Tathagata, thus spoke to that Bhikshu:

"Do you by yourself, O Bhikshu, know the perfection of all excellences and good qualities of a Buddha country?"

'He said: "O Bhagavat, I could not do this, but the Bhagavat alone. Explain the perfection of the excellences and all the good qualities of Buddha countries of the other Tathagatas, after hearing which we may fulfil everyone of their signs."

"Then, O Ananda, the Tathagata Lokesvararaja, holy and fully enlightened, knowing the good disposition of that Bhikshu, taught for a full koti of years the perfection of all the excellences and good qualities of Buddha countries belonging to eighty-one hundred thousand niyutas of kotis of Buddhas, together with the signs, indication, and description, desiring welfare, wishing for benefits, compassionate, full of compassion, so that there might never be an end of Buddha countries, having conceived great pity for all beings. The measure of life of that Tathagata was full forty kalpas.

'Then, O Ananda, that Bhikshu Dharmakara, taking the perfections of all the excellences and good qualities of those Buddha countries, of those eighty-one hundred thousand niyutas of kotis of Buddhas, and concentrating them all on one Buddha country, worshipped with his head

Maitreya Buddha

the feet of the Bhagavat Lokesvararaja, the Tathagata, turned respectfully round him to the right, and walked away from the presence of this Bhagavat. And afterwards, for the space of five kalpas, he thus concentrated the perfection of all the excellences and good qualities of the Buddha countries, such as had never been known before in the ten quarters of the whole world, more excellent, and more perfect than any, and composed the most excellent prayer.

'Thus, O Ananda, that Bhikshu concentrated in his mind the perfection of a Buddha country eighty-one times more immeasurable, noble, and excellent than the perfection of the eighty-one hundred thousand niyutas of kotis of Buddha countries that had been told to him by the Bhagavat Lokesvararaja, the Tathagata. And then, proceeding to where the Tatha.gata was, he worshipped the feet of the Bhagavat with his head, and said: "O Bhagavat, the perfection of all the excellences and good qualities of the Buddha countries has been concentrated by me."

'After this, O Ananda, the Tathagata Lokesvararaja thus spoke to the Bhikshu: " Preach then, O Bhikshu;—the Tathagata allows it. Now is the proper time, O Bhikshu. Delight the assembly, produce joy, let the lion's voice be heard, so that now and hereafter, noble-minded Bodhisattvas, hearing it, may comprehend the different subjects or occasions of the prayers for the perfection of the good qualities of a Buddha country."

'Then, O Ananda, that Bhikshu Dharmakara thus spoke at that time to the Bhagavat: "May the Bhagavat thus listen to me, to what my own prayers are, and how, after I shall have obtained the highest perfect knowledge, my own Buddha country will then be endowed with all inconceivable excellences and good qualities.

"O Bhagavat, if in that Buddha country of mine there should be either hell, brute-creation (birth as animals), the realm of departed spirits, or the body of Asuras, then may I not obtain the highest perfect knowledge.

"O Bhagavat, if in that Buddha country of mine the beings who are born there should fall away and die, and fall into hell, the brute-creation, the realm of departed spirits, or into the body of Asuras, then may I not obtain the highest perfect knowledge.

"O Bhagavat, if in that Buddha country of mine the beings who are born there should. not all be of one colour, a golden colour, then may I not obtain the highest perfect knowledge.

"O Bhagavat, if in that Buddha country of mine there should be perceived any difference between gods and men, except when people count and tell, saying: "These are gods and men, but only in ordinary and imperfect parlance," then may I not obtain the highest perfect knowledge.

"O Bhagavat, if in that Buddha country of mine the beings who are born there should not be possessed of the highest Paramitas of miraculous power and self-control, so that they could at least in the shortest moment of one thought step over a hundred thousand niyutas of kotis of Buddha countries, then may I not obtain the highest perfect knowledge.

"O Bhagavat, if in that Buddha country of mine the beings who are born there should not all be possessed of the recollection of their former births, so as at least to remember a hundred thousand niyutas of kotis of kalpas, then may I not obtain the highest perfect knowledge.

"O Bhagavat, if in that Buddha country of mine the beings who are born there should not all acquire the divine eye, so as at least to be able to see a hundred thousand niyutas of kotis of worlds, then may I not obtain the highest perfect knowledge.

"O Bhagavat, if in that Buddha country of mine the beings who are born there should not all acquire the divine ear, so as at least to be able to hear at the same time the good Law from a hundred thousand niyutas of kotis of

Buddha countries, then may I not obtain the highest perfect knowledge.

"O Bhagavat, if in that Buddha country of mine the beings, who are born there should not all be skilled in the knowledge of the thoughts of other people, so as at least to be able to know the deeds and thoughts of beings belonging to a hundred thousand niyutas of kotis of Buddha countries, then may I not obtain the highest perfect knowledge.

"O Bhagavat, if in that Buddha country of mine the beings who are born there should form any idea of property, even with regard to their own body, then may I not obtain the highest perfect knowledge.

'O Bhagavat, if in that Buddha country of mine the beings who are born there should not all be firmly established in absolute truth, till they have reached Mahaparinirvana, then may I not obtain the highest perfect knowledge.

"O Bhagavat, if any being should be able to count the pupils belonging to me after I have obtained the highest perfect knowledge in that Buddha country of mine, even if all beings who are contained in those three millions of spheres of the worlds, after having become Pratyeka-buddhas, should be counting for a hundred thousand niyutas of kotis of kalpas, then may I not obtain the highest perfect knowledge.

"O Bhagavat, if, after I have obtained the highest perfect knowledge, my light should be liable to be measured in this Buddha country of mine, even by the measure of a hundred thousand niyutas of kotis of Buddha countries, then may I not obtain the highest perfect knowledge.

"O Bhagavat, if the measure of the life of the beings in that Buddha country of mine, after I have obtained the highest perfect knowledge, should be liable to be measured, excepting always by their own power of prayer, then may I not obtain the highest perfect knowledge.

"O Bhagavat, if the measure of my life after I have obtained Bodhi should be limited, even by numbering a hundred thousand niyutas of kotis of kalpas, then may I not obtain the highest perfect knowledge.

"O Bhagavat, if, for the beings in this Buddha country of mine, after I have obtained Bodhi, even the name of sin should exist, then may I not obtain the highest perfect knowledge.

"O Bhagavat, if immeasurable and innumerable blessed Buddhas in immeasurable Buddha countries do not glorify my name, after I have obtained the Bodhi knowledge; if they do not preach my fame and proclaim my praise, and utter it together, then may I not obtain the highest perfect knowledge.

"O Bhagavat, if those beings who have directed their thought towards the highest perfect knowledge in other worlds, and who, after having heard my name, when I have obtained the Bodhi knowledge, have meditated on me with serene thoughts; if at the moment of their death, after having approached them, surrounded by an assembly of Bhikshus, I should not stand before them, worshipped by them, that is, so that their thoughts should not be troubled; then may I not obtain the highest perfect knowledge.

"O Bhagavat, if those beings who in immeasurable and innumerable Buddha countries, after they have heard my name, when I shall have obtained Bodhi, should direct their thought to be born in that Buddha country of mine, and should for that purpose bring their stock of merit to maturity, if these should not be born in that Buddha country, even those who have only ten times repeated the thought of that Buddha country, barring always those beings who have committed the five Anantarya sins and who have caused an obstruction and abuse of the good Law, then may I not obtain the highest perfect knowledge.

"O Bhagavat, if those beings who have been born in that Buddha country of mine, after I have obtained Bodhi, should not all be bound to one birth only, before reaching the highest perfect knowledge, barring always the special prayers of those very noble-minded Bodhisattvas who have put on the whole armour; of the Law who understand the welfare of all beings, who are devoted to all beings, who work for the attainment of Nirvana of all beings, who wish to perform the duty of a Bodhisattva in all worlds, who wish to serve all Buddhas, and to bring beings, in number like grains of sand of the river Ganga, to the highest perfect knowledge, and who besides are turned towards the higher practice, and perfect in the practice of the Samantabhadra discipline, then may I not obtain the highest perfect knowledge.

"O Bhagavat, if the Bodhisattvas who are born in that Buddha country of mine, after I have obtained Bodhi, should not all be able, after having gone to other Buddha countries, after their one morning-meal, to worship many hundreds of Buddhas, many thousands of Buddhas, many hundred thousands of Buddhas, many kotis of Buddhas, etc., till up to many hundred thousand niyutas of kotis of Buddhas, with objects which give every kind of pleasure, and this through the grace of the Buddha, then may I not obtain the highest perfect knowledge.

"O Bhagavat, if those Bodhisattvas in that Buddha country of mine, after I have obtained Bodhi, should wish their stock of merit to grow in the following shapes, either in gold, in silver, in jewels, in pearls, in beryls, in shells, in stones, in corals, in crystal, in amber, in red pearls, in diamond, etc., or in anyone of the other jewels or in all kinds of perfumes, in flowers, in garlands, in ointment, in incense-powder, in cloaks, in umbrellas, in flags, in banners, or in lamps; or in all kinds of dancing, singing, and music;—and if such gifts should not appear for them, from being produced as soon as thought of, then may I not obtain the highest perfect knowledge.

"O Bhagavat, if those beings who are born in that Buddha country of mine, after I have obtained Bodhi, should not all recite the story of the Law which is accompanied by omniscience, then may I not obtain the highest perfect knowledge.

"O Bhagavat, if the Bodhisattvas in that Buddha country of mine, after I have obtained Bodhi, should think thus: May we, remaining in this world, honour, revere, esteem, and worship the blessed Buddhas in immeasurable and innumerable Buddha countries, with cloaks, alms-bowls, beds, stools, refreshments, medicines, utensils, with flowers, incense, lamps, perfumes, garlands, ointment, powder, cloaks, umbrellas, flags, banners, with different kinds of dancing, singing, and music, and with showers of jewels—and if the blessed Buddhas should not accept them, when they are produced as soon as thought of, from compassion, then may I not obtain the highest perfect knowledge.

"O Bhagavat, if the Bodhisattvas who are born in that Buddha country of mine, after I have obtained Bodhi, should not all be in possession of strength of body as strong as the diamond (or thunderbolt) of Narayana, then may I not obtain the highest perfect knowledge.

"O Bhagavat, if any being in that Buddha country of mine, after I have obtained Bodhi, should learn the limit of the beauty of its ornament, even if he be possessed of the divine eye, and should know its various beauty, saying: "That Buddha country possesses so much beauty and so much magnificence," then may I not obtain the highest perfect knowledge.

"O Bhagavat, if in that Buddha country of mine, after I have obtained Bodhi, a Bodhisattva possessed even of a very small stock of merit, should not perceive the Bodhi-tree of noble beauty, at least a hundred yojanas in height, then may I not obtain the highest perfect knowledge.

"O Bhagavat, if in that Buddha country of mine, after I have obtained Bodhi, either teaching or learning should have to be made by any being, and they should not all be in possession of the perfect knowledge, then may I not obtain the highest perfect knowledge.

"O Bhagavat, if that Buddha country of mine, after I have obtained Bodhi, should not be so brilliant, that in it could be seen on all sides immeasurable, innumerable, inconceivable, incomparable, immense Buddha countries, as a round face is seen in a highly burnished round mirror, then may I not obtain the highest perfect knowledge.

"O Bhagavat, if in that Buddha country of mine, after I have obtained Bodhi, there should not be a hundred thousand of vases full of different sweet perfumes, made of all kinds of jewels, always smoking with incense, fit for the worship of Bodhisattvas and Tathagatas, rising into the sky beyond gods, men, and all things, then may I not obtain the highest perfect knowledge.

"O Bhagavat, if in that Buddha country of mine, after I have obtained Bodhi, there should not be showers of sweet jewel-flowers, always pouring down, and if there should not be sweet-sounding music-clouds, always playing, then may I not obtain the highest perfect knowledge.

"O Bhagavat, if the beings belonging to me, after I have obtained Bodhi, who are visible by their splendour, in immeasurable, innumerable, inconceivable, incomparable worlds, should not all be filled with pleasure, far beyond gods and men, then may I not obtain the highest perfect knowledge.

"O Bhagavat, if, after I have obtained Bodhi, the noble-minded Bodhisattvas in immeasurable, inconceivable, incomparable, immense Buddha countries on all sides, after having heard my name, should not be delivered from birth, through the merit arising from that hearing, and should not be strong in the knowledge of Dharanis, until they have obtained the very throne of Bodhi, then may I not obtain the highest perfect knowledge.

"O Bhagavat, if, after I have obtained Bodhi, women in immeasurable, innumerable, inconceivable, incomparable, immense Buddha countries on all sides, after having heard my name, should allow carelessness to arise, should not turn their thoughts towards Bodhi, should, when they are free from birth, not despise their female nature; and if they, being born again, should assume a second female nature, then may I not obtain the highest perfect knowledge.

"O Bhagavat, if, after I have obtained Bodhi, the Bodhisattvas who in immeasurable, innumerable, inconceivable, incomparable, immense Buddha countries round about in the ten quarters having heard my name, and having fallen down, shall worship me with prostrate reverence, should not, when performing the duty of Bodhisattvas, be honoured by the world and by the gods, then may I not obtain the highest perfect knowledge.

"O Bhagavat, if, after I have obtained Bodhi, the work of dyeing, sewing, drying, washing of his cloaks should have to be performed by any Bodhisattva, and they should not perceive themselves, as quick as thought, covered by newly-produced excellent cloaks, granted to them by the Tathagata, then may I not obtain the highest perfect knowledge.

"O Bhagavat, if the beings who are born at the same time in that Buddha country, after I have obtained Bodhi, should not obtain such happiness as that of the holy Bhikshu who is free from pain and has obtained the third meditation, then may I not obtain the highest perfect knowledge.

"O Bhagavat, if those Bodhisattvas who are born in that Buddha country of mine, after I have obtained Bodhi, should not produce from different jewel-trees such a mass of excellent ornaments in that Buddha country, as they should wish for, then may I not obtain the highest perfect knowledge.

"O Bhagavat, if the Bodhisattvas who are born in other Buddha countries, when they have heard my name, after I shall have obtained Bodhi, should suffer any diminution in the strength of their senses, then may I not obtain the highest perfect knowledge.

"O Bhagavat, if, after I have obtained Bodhi, the Bodhisattvas, from hearing my name in a place of a different Buddha country, should not obtain the Samadhi called Suvibhaktavati, in which Samadhi the Bodhisattvas will see immeasurable, innumerable, inconceivable, incomparable, immense, blessed Buddhas one moment after another; and if that Samadhi of theirs should come to an end meanwhile, then may I not obtain the highest perfect knowledge.

"O Bhagavat, if, after I have obtained Bodhi, beings, having heard my name in Buddha countries different from this, should not, through the stock of merit which follows on that hearing, obtain birth in a noble family, till they arrive at Bodhi, then may I not obtain the highest perfect knowledge.

"O Bhagavat, if, after I have obtained Bodhi, the Bodhisattvas who live in other Buddha countries, after hearing my name, till they have reached Bodhi by the stock of merit which follows on that hearing, should not all obtain a combination of their stock of merit with the joy and gladness of their Bodhisattva life, then may I not obtain the highest perfect knowledge.

"O Bhagavat, if, after I have obtained Bodhi, the Bodhisattvas, as soon as they have heard my name, in other worlds, should not obtain the Samadhi called Samantanugata, in which Bodhisattvas honour one moment after another immeasurable, innumerable, inconceivable, incomparable, immense, blessed Buddhas, and if that Samadhi of theirs should come to an end before they have reached the throne of Bodhi, then may I not obtain the highest perfect knowledge.

"O Bhagavat, if the beings who are born in the Buddha country of mine, after I have obtained Bodhi, should not hear, as quick as thought, such a teaching of the Law as they wish to hear, then may I not obtain the highest perfect knowledge.

"O Bhagavat, if, after I have obtained Bodhi, the Bodhisattvas in this and other Buddha countries, as soon as they have heard my name, should ever turn back from the highest perfect knowledge, then may I not obtain the highest perfect knowledge.

"O Bhagavat, if, after I have obtained Bodhi, and have become a Buddha-teacher, the Bodhisattvas who hear my name in Buddha countries, and obtain the first, the second, and the third degrees of endurance, as soon as they have heard my name, should turn away again from Buddha, the Law, and the Sangh, then may I not obtain the highest perfect knowledge."

'And again, O Ananda, when he had spoken such prayers, that Bhikshu Dharmakara, at that time, through the grace of Buddha spoke these verses:

"If, when I have obtained Bodhi, there should not be for me an excellent Pranidhana of such a character, then, O Prince, O best of beings, may I not be endowed with the ten powers, incomparable, worthy of offerings.

"If there should not be for me such a country, endowed with many and various mighty and divine endowments, I should gladly go to hell, suffering pain, and not be a king of treasures.

"If, when I have approached the Bodhi throne, my name should not quickly reach the ten quarters, the broad and many endless Buddha countries, may I not be a lord of the world, endowed with power.

"If indeed I should delight in the enjoyments of love, being deprived of zeal, understanding and prudence, even after having reached the incomparable and blessed Bodhi, may I not be a teacher in the world, endowed with power.

"The lord of vast light, incomparable and infinite, has illuminated all Buddha countries in all the quarters, he has quieted passions, all sins and errors, he has quieted the fire in the walk of hell.

"After making his broad eye lustrous, after driving away the darkness from all men, after removing all untimely misfortunes, he led hither those who dwell in heaven and who shine with endless light.

"The splendour of sun and moon does not shine in heaven, nor the fiery splendour of the maze of jewels of the gods; the Lord overcomes all splendour, he, the bright one, who has performed his former discipline.

"He is the best of men, the treasure of all who suffer; there is no one like him in all the quarters. Having completed a hundred thousand of good works, he, in his assembly, raised the lion-voice of Buddha.

"After having worshipped former self-existing Jinas, after having performed immeasurable kotis of vows and penances, he became in this, his best of spiritual existences, the best of beings, possessed of the full power of prayers.

"As the Bhagavat, the Lord, who is possessed of unlimited light of knowledge, knows the three kinds of knowledge in the world, may I also be worthy of equal offerings, the best of sages, the leader of men.

"If, O Lord, this my prayer succeeds, after I have obtained Bodhi, may this sphere of a thousand worlds tremble, and may a shower of flowers descend on the hosts of gods."

'Then the earth trembled, flowers were showered down, hundreds of instruments resounded in the sky, powder of heavenly sweet sandalwood was scattered, and there was a voice saying: "Thou wilt be a Buddha in the world."

'That Bhikshu Dharmakara, the nobleminded Bodhisattva, O Ananda, was possessed of this perfection of prayers. And a few Bodhisattvas only, O Ananda, are possessed of such a perfection of prayers. There is on this earth an appearance of a few only of such prayers. Of a few, however, existence cannot be denied.

'Then again, O Ananda, this Bhikshu Dharmakara having recited these peculiar prayers before the Bhagavat Lokesvararaja, the Tathagata, and before the world including gods, Mara, and Brahma, and before people consisting of Sramanas and Brahmins with gods, men, and Asuras, was esablished in the attainment of the true promise. And proclaiming this purity of the Buddha country, this greatness and excellence of the Buddha country, and performing the duty of a Bodhisattva, he never conceived the remotest thoughts of lust, malevolence, and cruelty, during a hundred thousand niyutas of kotis of years, immeasurable, innumerable, inconceivable, incomparable, measureless, immense, inexpressible; and he never conceived the idea of lust, malevolence, and

Manjushree Buddha

cruelty, nay, he never conceived the idea of form, sound, smell, taste, and touch. He was gentle, charming indeed, and compassionate; pleasant to live with, agreeable, amiable, content, of few wishes, satisfied, retired, not evil, not foolish, not suspicious, not crooked, not wicked, not deceitful, tender, kindly speaking, always zealous, docile in the searching after the pure Law. And for the good of all beings, he recited the great prayer, showing respect to friends, teachers, masters, the Sangh, the Law, and Buddha, always girded for the performance of the duties of the Bodhisattva, righteous, gentle, not deceitful, not flattering, virtuous, a leader for the sake of rousing others to perform all good laws, producing by his activity the ideas of emptiness, causelessness, and purposelessness, and he was well guarded in his speech. Then, performing the duties of a Bodhisattva, after having given up all speaking which, when spoken, serves to injure one's self or others or both, he employed only such speech as served the pleasure and benefit of himself, others, or both. And he was so wise that, 'when entering into capitals, kingdoms, countries, towns, cities, and villages, he was always perfectly restrained with regard to all objects of sense. Performing himself the duties of the Bodhisattva without interruption, he walked himself in the highest perfection, Paramita of liberality, and he also roused others to walk in the same. And himself walking in the highest perfections of knowledge, meditation, strength, patience, and virtue, he roused others also to walk in the same. And he has collected so large a stock of merit that, wherever he is born, there arise for him many hundreds of thousands of niyutas of kotis of treasures from out of the earth.

'By him, while he was thus performing the duties of a Bodhisattva, immeasurable and innumerable hundreds of thousands of niyutas of kotis of beings were established in perfect enlightenment, of whom it is not easy to know the limit by means of speech. So many immeasurable and innumerable holy Buddhas were honoured, revered, esteemed, and worshipped, and enabled to touch whatever causes pleasure, such as cloaks, alms-bowls, couches, seats, refreshments, medicines, and other furniture. It is not easy to know the limit by pointing it out in works, as to how many beings were established by him in the noble families of Brahmins, Kshatriyas, ministers, house-holders, and merchants. In the same manner they were established in the sovereignty of Jambudvipa (India), and they were established in the character of Chakravartins, Lokapalas, Sakras, Suyamas, Sutushitas, Sunirmitas, Vasavartins, Devarajas, and Mahabrahmins. So many immeasurable and innumerable Buddhas were honoured, revered, esteemed, and worshipped, and requested to turn the wheel of the Law, of whom it is not easy to know the limit by means of words.

'And he collected such virtue, that out of his mouth, while performing the duties of a Bodhisattva, during immeasurable, innumerable, inconceivable, incomparable, immense, measureless, inexpressible kotis of kalpas, there breathed a sweet and more than heavenly smell of sandalwood. From all the pores of his hair there arose the smell of lotus, and he was pleasing to everybody, gracious and beautiful, endowed with the fulness of the best bright colour. As his body was adorned with all the good signs and marks, there arose from the pores of his hair and from the palms of his hands all sorts of precious ornaments in the shape of all kinds of cloaks and vestments, in the shape of all kinds of flowers, incense, scents, garlands, ointments, umbrellas, flags, and banners, and in the shape of all kinds of instrumental music. And there appeared also, streaming forth from the palms of his hands, all kinds of viands and drink, food, hard and soft, and sweetmeats, and all kinds of enjoyments and pleasures. Thus then that Bhikshu Dharmakara, O Ananda, had obtained the command of all necessaries, after performing the duties of a Bodhisattva.'

After this, the blessed Ananda thus spoke to the Bhagavat: 'O Bhagavat, has that Bhikshu Dharmakara, the noble-minded Bodhisattva, after having obtained the highest perfect knowledge, passed away, having entered Nirvana, or has he not yet been enlightened, or is he now living and enlightened, and does he dwell now, remain, support himself, and teach the Law?'

The Bhagavat said: 'Not indeed, O Ananda, has that Tathagata passed away, nor has he not yet come, but the Tathagata, the holy, after having obtained the highest perfect knowledge, dwells now, remains, supports himself, and teaches the Law, in the western quarter, in the Buddha country, distant from this world by a hundred thousand niyutas of kotis of Buddha countries, in the world which is called Sukhavati, being called Amitabha, the Tathagata, holy and fully enlightened. He is surrounded by innumerable Bodhisattvas, and worshipped by endless Sravakas, and in possession of the endless perfection of his Buddha country.

'And his light is immeasurable, so that it is not easy to know the limit of its measure, saying, he stands illuminating so many hundreds of Buddha countries, so many thousands of Buddha countries, so many hundred thousands of Buddha countries, so many kotis of Buddha countries, so many hundred kotis of Buddha countries, so many thousand kotis of Buddha countries, so many hundred thousands of kotis of Buddha countries, so many hundred thousands of niyutas of kotis of Buddha countries. But indeed, O Ananda, to put it briefly, a hundred thousand niyutas of kotis of Buddha countries, equal to the sands of the river Ganga, are always lighted up in the eastern quarter, by the light of that Bhagavat Amitabha. Thus on every side in the southern, western, northern quarter, in the zenith and nadir, in every one of these quarters, there are a hundred thousand niyutas of kotis of Buddha countries, like the sands of the river Ganga, always lighted up by the light of that Bhagavat Amitabha, excepting the Buddhas, the Bhagavats, who, through the practice of their former prayers, have lighted up the world by their own light, which is a fathom in length, or by their light which is one, two, three, four, five, ten, twenty, thirty, forty, or fifty yojanas in length, or a hundred or thousand or hundred thousand yojanas in length, until their brightness reaches many hundred thousand niyutas of kotis of yojanas in length. There is not, O Ananda, any case of likeness, by which the extent of the light of that Tathagata Amitabha could be understood. Hence, O Ananda, for that reason that Tathagata is called Amitabha possessed of infinite light and he is called Amitaprabha possessed of infinite splendour, Amitaprabhasa possessed of infinite brilliancy, Asamaptaprabha, whose light is never finished, Asangataprabha, whose light is not conditioned, Prabhasikhotsrishtaprabha, whose light proceeds from flames of light, Sadivyamaniprabha, whose light is that of heavenly jewels, Apratihatarasmiragaprabha, whose light has the colour of unimpeded rays, Rajaniyaprabha, possessed of beautiful light, Premaniyaprabha, possessed of lovely light, Pramodaniyaprabha, possessed of delightful light, Sangamaniyaprabha, possessed of attractive light, Uposhaniyaprabha, possessed of pleasant light, Anibandhaniyaprabha, possessed of light that cannot be stopped, Ativiryaprabha, possessed of extremely powerful light, Atulyaprabha, possessed of incomparable light, Abhibhuyanarendrabhutrayendraprabha, possessed of light greater than that of the lords of men, may, the lords of the three worlds, Srantasanchayendusuryajihmikaranaprabha, possessed of light which bends the full moon and the sun, Abhibhuyalokapalasakrabrahmasuddhavasamahesvarasarvajihmikaranaprabha, possessed of light which bends all the conquered gods, Mahesvara, the Suddhavasas, Brahma, Sakra, and the Lokapalas.

'This splendour of the Arya (noble) is pure, great, producing bodily pleasure, happiness of mind, producing happiness, delight, and joy for men and not men, Kinnaras, Maharajas, Garudas, Gandharvas, Yakshas, Nagas, Asuras, and Devas; and producing the pleasure of beings of good disposition.

'And in this manner, O Ananda, the Tathagata might speak for a whole kalpa on the work of the Tathagata

Amitabha, beginning with his light, and yet he would not be able to reach the end of the virtues of that light of that Tathagata, neither would there be any failure of the self-confidence in the Tathagata himself. And why? Because, O Ananda, both these things are immeasurable, innumerable, inconceivable, and endless, first, the greatness of the excellence of the light of that Tathagata Amitabha, the Bhagavat, and secondly, the unsurpassed light of the knowledge possessed by the Tathagata, by myself.

'And, O Ananda, the assembly of the hearers of that Tathagata Amitabha is immeasurable, so that it is not easy to learn its measure, so as to be able to say, there are so many kotis of the hearers, so many hundreds, thousands, hundred-thousands, kankaras, vimbaras, niyutas, akshobhyas, vivahas, srwtas, ojas, so many periods, called immeasurable, innumerable, countless, incomparable, inconceivable. Now, for instance, O Ananda, the Bhikshu Maudgalyayana, having obtained miraculous power, might, if he wished, count in one day and night, how many kinds of stars there are in the universal world. Then, let there be a hundred thousand niyutas of kotis of such men, endowed with miraculous powers, and let them do nothing else but count the first company only of the hearers of the Tathagata Amitabha, during hundred thousand niyutas of kotis of years, and yet by them thus counting even the hundredth part would not be counted, even the thousandth, even the hundred thousandth, nay, not even so far as the minutest part, or likeness, or approach towards it would have been counted.

'Thus, for instance, O Ananda, a man might throw out from the great ocean, which is not to be measured across by less than eighty-four thousand yojanas, one single drop of water by the sharp end of hair, which is divided a hundred times. What do you think then, Ananda, —which would be greater, one drop of water which has been thrown up by the sharp pointed hair divided a hundred times, or the mass of water left in the great ocean?'

Ananda said: 'Even a thousand yojanas, O Bhagavat, would be a small portion of the great ocean, how much more then one drop of water thrown out by a sharp pointed hair divided a hundred times!'

Bhagavat said: 'As that one drop of water, exactly so large (so small in proportion) was the first company of the hearers. And let there be reckoning made by those Bhikshus, who are like Maudgalyayana, counting for a hundred thousand niyutas of kotis of years, and yet, as to the mass of water left in the great ocean, it would even then have to be considered as not counted. How much more with regard to the second, third, and the rest of the companies of the hearers! Therefore, the mass of hearers of the Bhagavat is endless and boundless, and receives the name of "immeasurable and innumerable."

'And, O Ananda, the length of the life of that Bhagavat Amitabha, the Tathagata, is immeasurable, so that it is not easy to know its length, so as to be able to say that it comprises, so many hundreds of kalpas, so many thousands of kalpas, so many hundred thousands of kalpas, so many kotis of kalpas, so many hundreds of kotis of kalpas, so many thousands of kotis of kalpas, so many hundred thousands of kotis of kalpas, so many hundred thousands of niyutas of kotis of kalpas. Therefore, O Ananda, the limit of the measure of the life of that Bhagavat is immeasurable indeed. Therefore, that Tathagata is called Amitayus.

'And as, O Ananda, the rule of making known the reckoning of kalpas exists here in this world, ten kalpas have passed now since Bhagavat Amitayus, the Tathagata, arose and awoke to the highest perfect knowledge.

'And, O Ananda, the world called Sukhavati belonging to that Bhagavat Amitabha is prosperous, rich, good to live in, fertile, lovely, and filled with many gods and men. Then, O Ananda, in that world there are neither hells, nor the brute creation, nor the realm of departed spirits, nor bodies of Asuras, nor untimely births. And there do not appear in this world such gems as are known in the world Sukhavati.

'Now, O Ananda, that world Sukhavati is fragrant with several sweet-smelling scents, rich in manifold flowers and fruits, adorned with gem trees, and frequented by tribes of manifold sweet-voiced birds, which have been made by the Tathagata on purpose. And, O Ananda, those gem trees are of several colours, of many colours, and of many hundred thousand colours. There are gem trees there of golden colour, and made of gold. There are those of silver colour, and made of silver. There are those of beryl colour, and made of beryl. There are those of crystal colour, and made of crystal. There are those of coral colour, and made of coral. There are those of red pearl colour, and made of red pearls. There are those of diamond colour, and made of diamonds.

'There are some trees of two gems, gold and silver. There are some of three gems, gold, silver, and beryl. There are some of four gems, gold, silver, beryl, and crystal. There are some of five gems, gold, silver, beryl, crystal, and coral. There are some of six gems, gold, silver, beryl, crystal, coral, and red pearls. There are some of seven gems, gold, silver, beryl, crystal, coral, red pearls, and diamonds as the seventh.

'And there, O Ananda, of the trees made of gold, the flowers, leaves, small branches, branches, trunks, and roots are made of gold, and the fruits are made of silver. Of trees made of silver, the flowers, leaves, small branches, branches, trunks, and roots are made of silver only, and the fruits are made of beryl. Of trees made of beryl, the flowers, leaves, small branches, branches, trunks, and roots are made of beryl, and the fruits are made of crystal. Of trees made of crystal, the flowers, leaves, small branches, branches, trunks, and roots are made of crystal only, and the fruits are made of coral. Of trees made of coral, the flowers, leaves, small branches, branches, trunks, and roots are made of coral only, and the fruits are made of red pearls. Of trees made of red pearls, the flowers, leaves, small branches, branches, trunks, and roots are made of red pearls only, and the fruits are made of diamonds. Of trees made of diamonds, the flowers, leaves, small branches, branches, trunks, and roots are made of diamonds only, and the fruits are made of gold.

'Of some trees, O Ananda, the roots are made of gold, the trunks of silver, the branches of beryl, the small branches of crystal, the leaves of coral, the flowers of red pearls, and the fruits of diamonds. Of some trees, O Ananda, the roots are made of silver, the trunks of beryl, the branches of crystal, the small branches of coral, the leaves of red pearls, the flowers of diamonds, and the fruits of gold. Of some trees, O Ananda, the roots are made of beryl, the trunks of crystal, the branches of coral, the small branches of red pearls, the leaves of diamond, the flowers of gold, and the fruits of silver. Of some trees, O Ananda, the roots are made of crystal, the trunks of coral, the branches of red pearls, the small branches of diamonds, the leaves of gold, the flowers of silver, and the fruits of beryl. Of some trees, O Ananda, the roots are made of coral, the trunks of red pearls, the branches of diamonds, the small branches of gold, the leaves of silver, the flowers of beryl, and the fruits of crystal. Of some trees, O Ananda, the roots are made of red pearls, the trunks of diamonds, the branches of gold, the small branches of silver, the leaves of beryl, the flowers of crystal, and the fruits of coral. Of some trees, O Ananda, the roots are made of diamonds, the trunks of gold, the branches of silver, the small branches of beryl, the leaves of crystal, the flowers of coral, and the fruits of red pearls. Of some trees, O Ananda, the roots are made of the seven gems, the trunks of the seven gems, the branches of the seven gems, the small branches of the seven gems, the leaves of the seven gems, the flowers of the seven gems, and the fruits of the seven gems.

'And, O Ananda, the roots, trunks, branches, small branches, leaves, flowers, and fruits of all those trees are pleasant to touch, and fragrant. And, when those trees are moved by the wind, a sweet and delightful sound proceeds from them, never tiring, and never disagreeable to hear. That Buddha country, O Ananda, is always on every side surrounded by such trees made of the seven gems, by masses of Kadali banana trees, and rows of palm, trees, made of the seven gems, and entirely surrounded with golden nets, and wholly covered with lotus flowers, made of all kinds of gems.

'There are lotus flowers there, half a yojana in circumference. There are others, one yojana in circumference; and others, two, three, four, or five yojanas in circumference; nay, there are some, as much as ten yojanas in circumference. And from each gem-lotus there proceed thirty-six hundred thousand kotis of rays of light. And from each ray of light there proceed thirty-six hundred thousand kotis of Buddhas, with bodies of golden colour, possessed of the thirty-two marks of great men, who go and teach the Law to beings in the immeasurable and innumerable worlds in the eastern quarter. Thus also in the southern, western, and northern quarters, above and below, in the cardinal and intermediate points, they go their way to the immeasurable and innumerable worlds and teach the Law to beings in the whole world.

'And again, O Ananda, there are no black mountains anywhere in that Buddha country, nor anywhere jewel mountains, nor anywhere Sumerus, kings of mountains, nor anywhere Chakravadas, great Chakravadas, kings of mountains. And that Buddha country is level on every side, lovely, like the palm of the hand, with districts full of jewels and treasures of every kind.'

After this, the blessed Ananda spoke thus to the Bhagavat: 'But in that case, O Bhagavat, where do the gods consisting of the companies of the four Maharjas who dwell on the side of the Sumeru, and where do the Tayastrimsa gods who dwell on the top of the Sumeru, find their place?'

Bhagavat said: 'What do you think, O Ananda, where do these other beings find their place, who in this world dwell above the king of mountains, Sumeru, namely, the

Yamadevas, Tushitas, Nirmanaratis, Paranirmitava-savartins, Brahmakayikas, Brahmapurohitas, Mahabrahmins, as far as the Akanishthas?'

Ananda replied: 'O Bhagavat, the result of works and the outcome of works are inconceivable.'

Bhagavat said: 'Here, you see, the result of works and the outcome of works are inconceivable. But to the blessed Buddhas the position of Buddhas is not inconceivable, while to thee the holy and miraculous power of virtuous beings, whose stock of merit has become ripened, seems inconceivable.'

Ananda said: 'I had no doubt on this, no difference of opinion, or hesitation; on the contrary, I ask only the Tathagata about this matter in order to destroy the doubts, the differences of opinion, and the hesitations of future beings.'

Bhagavat said: 'All right, Ananda, this is what you ought to do.

'In that world Sukhavati, O Ananda, there flow different kinds of rivers; there are great rivers there, one yojana in breadth; there are rivers up to twenty, thirty, forty, fifty yojanas in breadth, and up to twelve yojanas in depth. All these rivers are delightful, carrying water of different sweet odour, carrying bunches of flowers adorned with various gems, resounding with sweet voices. And, O Ananda, there proceeds from an instrument which consists of hundred thousand kotis of parts, which embodies heavenly music and is played by clever people, the same delightful sound which proceeds from those great rivers, the sound which is deep, unknown, incomprehensible, clear, pleasant to the ear, touching the heart, beloved, sweet, delightful, never tiring, never disagreeable, pleasant to hear, as if it always said, "Non-eternal, peaceful, unreal." Such a sound comes to be heard by these beings.

'And again, O Ananda, the borders of those great rivers on both sides are filled with jewel trees of various scents, from which bunches of flowers, leaves, and branches of all kinds hang down. And if the beings, who are on the borders of those rivers, wish to enjoy sport full of heavenly delights, the water rises to the ankle only after they have stepped into the rivers, if they wish it to be so; or if they wish it, the water rises to their knees, to their hips, to their sides, and to their ears. And heavenly pleasures arise. Again, if the beings then wish the water to be cold, it is cold; if they wish it to be hot, it is hot; if they wish it to be hot and cold, it is hot and cold, according to their pleasure.

'And those great rivers flow along, full of water scented with the best perfumes of the Uragasara sandalwood, of Tagaras, Kalanusarin, dark, fragrant sandalwood, trees, Agarus, and heavenly Tamalapatras; covered with flowers of the white water lilies, and heavenly Utpalas, Padmas, Kumudas, and Pundarikas; full of delightful sounds of peacocks, sparrows, kunalas, cuckoos, sarikas, parrots, ducks, geese, herons, cranes, swans and others; with small islands inhabited by flocks of birds, created by the Tathagata; adorned with fields, full of metals; with fjords on which it is easy to drink, free from mud, and covered with gold dust. And when these beings there desire, thinking what kind of wishes should be fulfilled for them, then exactly such wishes are fulfilled for them according to the Law.

'And, O Ananda, the sound which rises from that water is delightful, and the whole Buddha eountry is aroused by it. And if beings, who stand on the borders of the river, wish that the sound should not come within their ear-shot, then it does not come within their ear-shot, even if they are possessed of the heavenly ear. And whatever sound a man wishes to hear, exactly that delightful sound he hears, as for instance, the sound "Buddha, Dharma, Sangha, the Paramitas, highest perfections, the Bhumis, stages, the Balas, powers, Vaisaradya, perfections, Avenikabuddhadharma, freedom from attachment, Pratisamvit, consciousness; Sunyata, emptiness, Animitta, unconditioned, Apranihita, free from desire, Anabhisamskara, not made, Ajata, not born, Anutpada, without

Lord Buddha, Thailand

origin, Abhava, not being, and Nirodha, cessation; Santa, prasanta, and upasanta, peace; Mahamaitri, great love, Mahakaruna, great pity, Mahamudita, great rejoicing, and Mahopeksha, great forgiveness; Anutpattika-dharmakshanti, resignation to consequences which have not yet arisen, and Abhishekabhumipratilambha, attainment of the royal stages."

'And having heard these sounds, everybody feels the highest delight and pleasure accompanied by retirement, passionlessness, quiet, cessation, law, and a stock of merit leading to the perfect knowledge.

'And, O Ananda, there is nowhere in that Sukhavati world any sound of sin, obstacle, misfortune, distress, and destruction; there is nowhere any sound of pain, even the sound of perceiving what is neither pain nor pleasure is not there, O Ananda, how much less the sound of pain! For that reason, O Ananda, that world is called Sukhavati, shortly, but not in full. For, O Ananda, the whole kalpa would come to an end, while the different causes of the pleasure of the world Sukhavati are being praised, and even then the end of those causes of happiness could not be reached.

'And again, O Ananda, the beings, who have been and will be born in that world Sukhavati, will be endowed with such colour, strength, vigour, height and breadth, dominion, accumulation of virtue; with such enjoyments of dress, ornaments, gardens, palaces, and pavilions; and such enjoyments of touch, taste, smell, and sound; in fact with all enjoyments and pleasures, exactly like the Paranirmitavasavartin gods.

'And again, O Ananda, in that world Sukhavati, beings do not take food consisting of gross materials of gravy or molasses; but whatever food they desire, such food they perceive, as if it were taken, and become delighted in body and mind. Yet they need not put it into their mouth.

'And if, after they are satisfied, they wish different kinds of perfumes, then with these very heavenly kinds of perfumes the whole Buddha country is scented. And whosoever wishes to perceive there such perfume, every perfume of every scent of the Gandharvaraja does always reach his nose.

'And in the same manner, if they desire musical instruments, banners, flags, umbrellas, cloaks, powders, ointments, garlands, and scents, then the whole Buddha country shines with such things. If they desire cloaks of different colours and many hundred thousand colours, then with these very best cloaks the whole Buddha country shines. And the people feel themselves covered with them.

'And if they desire such ornaments, as for instance, head-ornaments, ear-ornaments, neck-ornaments, hand and foot ornaments, namely, diadems, earrings, bracelets, armlets, necklaces, chains, ear-jewels, seals, gold strings, girdles, gold nets, pearl nets, jewel nets, nets of bells made of gold and jewels, then they see that Buddha country shining with such ornaments adorned with many hundred thousand jewels, that are fastened to ornament trees. And they perceive themselves to be adorned with these ornaments.

'And if they desire a palace, with colours and emblems of such and such height and width, adorned with hundred thousand gates made with different jewels, covered with different heavenly flowers, full of couches strewn with beautiful cushions, then exactly such a palace appears before them. And in these delightful palaces they dwell, play, sport, walk about, being honoured, and surrounded by seven times seven thousands of Apsarases.

'And in that world, there is no difference between gods and men, except when they are spoken of in ordinary and imperfect parlance as gods and men. And, O Ananda, as a low man and impotent man, before the face of the mighty king, is neither bright, nor warm, nor brilliant, nor is he self-confident and radiant, thus Sakra, king of the Devas, if before the face of the Paranirmitavasavartin gods, is neither bright, nor warm, nor brilliant, namely, with regard to his gardens, palaces, dresses, ornaments, his dominion, his perfection, his miraculous power, or his supremacy, his comprehension of the Law, and his full enjoyment of the Law. And, O Ananda, as the Paranirmitavasavartin gods are there, thus men must be considered in the world Sukhavati.

'And again, O Ananda, in that world Sukhavati, when the time of forenoon has come, the winds are greatly agitated and blowing everywhere in the four quarters. And they shake and drive many beautiful, graceful, and many-coloured stalks of the gem trees, which are perfumed with sweet heavenly scents, so that many hundred beautiful flowers of delightful scent fall down on the great earth, which is all full of jewels. And with these flowers that Buddha country is adorned on every side seven fathoms deep. As a clever man might spread out a flower-bed on the earth and make it even with both his hands, beautiful and charming, even thus with those flowers of various scents and colours that Buddha country is shining on every side seven fathoms deep. And these many flowers are soft, pleasant to touch, if one may use a comparison, like Kachilindika (some kind of soft substance). If one puts one's foot on them, they sink down four inches; if one raises one's foot, they rise again four inches. When the time of the forenoon has gone again, these flowers vanish without leaving anything behind. Then that Buddha country is again clean, pleasant, beautiful, and without fading flowers. The winds blow again everywhere in the four quarters, and scatter down fresh flowers as before. And as it is in the forenoon, so it is at noon, at twilight, in the first, middle, and last watch of the night. And the beings, if touched by those winds which blow perfume with various scents, are as full of happiness as a Bhikshu who has obtained Nirvana.

'And in that Buddha country, O Ananda, no mention is ever made of the names of fire, sun, moon, planets, Nakshatras, constellations, and stars, or of blinding darkness. There is no mention even of day and night, except in the conversation of the Tathagata. Nor is there any idea of predial property belonging to monasteries.

'And again, O Ananda, in that world Sukhavati at the proper time clouds full of heavenly perfumed water pour down heavenly flowers of all colours; heavenly seven jewels, heavenly sandalwood-powder, and heavenly umbrellas, flags, and banners are poured down. And in the sky, the heavenly flowers of all colours, and heavenly canopies are held, likewise heavenly excellent umbrellas and all kinds of ornaments, heavenly musical instruments are played, and heavenly Apsarases dance.

'And again, O Ananda, in that Buddha country whatever beings have been born, and are being born, and will be born, are always constant in absolute truth, till they have reached Nirvana. And why is that? Because there is no room or mention there of the other two divisions, such as beings not constant or constant in falsehood.

'On this wise, O Ananda, that world is briefly called Sukhavati, not at full length. Even a kalpa, O Ananda, would come to an end, while the causes of happiness which exist in that world Sukhavati are being praised, and yet it would be impossible to reach the end of them.'

Then the Bhagavat at that time spoke the following verses:

'Thus, O Ananda, the world Sukhavati is endowed with immeasurable good qualities and excellences.

'And again, O Ananda, in the ten quarters, and in each of them, in all the Buddha countries equal in number to the sand of the Ganga, the blessed Buddhas equal in number to the sand of the Ganga, glorify the name of the blessed Amitabha, the Tathagata, they preach his fame, they proclaim his glory, they extol his virtue. And why? Because all beings who hear the name of the blessed Amitabha, and having heard it, raise their thought with joyful longing, even for once only, will not turn away again from the highest perfect knowledge.

'And before the eyes of those beings, O Ananda, who again and again think of the Tathagata reverently, and who make the great and unmeasured stock of good works grow, turning their thought towards Bodhi, and who pray to be born in that world, Amitabha, the Tathagata, holy and fully enlightened, when the time of their death has approached, will appear, surrounded by many companies of Bhikshus and honoured by them. And then these beings, having seen the Bhagavat, their thoughts filled with joy, will, when they have died, be born in that world of Sukhavati. And if, O Ananda, any son or daughter of a good family should wish—What?—How then may I see that Tathagata Amitabha visibly, then he must raise his thought on to the highest perfect knowledge, he must direct his thought with perseverance and excessive desire towards that Buddha country, and direct the stock of his good works towards being born there.

'But before the eyes of those who do not care much about the Tathagata Amitabha, and who do not vigorously increase the great and unmeasured stock of their good works, the Tathagata Amitabha, holy and fully enlightened, will appear, at the time of death, with the company of Bhikshus, in breadth and height and form and beauty, very like the former, and very like the real Tathagata, but only created by thought. And they, through their meditation that dwells on perceiving the sight of the Tathagata, and with unfailing memory, will, when they have died, be born in the same Buddha country.

'And again, O Ananda, those beings who meditate on the Tathagata by giving him the ten thoughts, and who will direct their desire towards that Buddha country, and who will feel satisfaction when the profound doctrines are being preached, and who will not fall off, nor despair, nor fail, but will meditate on that Tathagata, if it were by one thought only, and will direct their desire toward that Buddha country, they also will see the Tathagata Amitabha, while they are in a dream, they will be born in the world Sukhavati, and will never turn away from the highest perfect knowledge.

'And, O Ananda, after thus seeing the cause and effect, the Tathagatas of the ten quarters, in immeasurable and innumerable worlds, glorify the name of the Tathagata Amitabha, preach his fame, and proclaim his praise. And again, O Ananda, in that Buddha country, Bodhisattvas equal in number to the sand of the Ganga approach, from the ten quarters, and in each quarter towards that Tathagata Amitabha, in order to see him, to bow before him, to worship him, to consult him, and likewise in order to see that company of Bodhisattvas, and the different kinds of perfection in the multitude of ornaments and excellences belonging to that Buddha country.'

Then at that time, the Bhagavat, in order to illustrate this matter in fuller measure, recited these verses:

'As there are Buddha countries equal to the sand of the river Ganga in the eastern quarter, whence all the Bodhisattvas come to worship the Buddha, the lord Amitayus;

'And they having taken many bunches of flowers of different colours, sweetly-scented and delightful, shower them down on the best leader of men, on Amitayus, worshipped by gods and men;

'In the same manner there are as many Buddha countries in the southern, western, and northern quarters, whence they come with the Bodhisattvas to worship the Buddha, the lord Amitayus.

'And they having taken many handfulls of scents of different colours, sweetly-scented and delightful, shower them down on the best leader of men, on Amitayus, worshipped by gods and men.

'These many Bodhisattvas having worshipped and revered the feet of Amitaprabha, and having walked round him respectfully, speak thus: "Oh, the country of Buddha shines wonderfully!"

'And they cover him again with handfulls of flowers, with thoughts jubilant, with incomparable joy, and proclaim their wish before that lord: "May our country also be such as this."

'And what was thrown there as handfulls of flowers arose in the form of an umbrella extending over a hundred yoganas, and the beautiful country shines and is well adorned, and flowers cover the whole body of Buddha.

'These Bodhisattvas having thus honoured him, how do they act?—Delighted they pronounce this speech: "Gains by those people are well gained, by whom the name of the best man has been heard.

' "By us also all the gain has been well gained, because we have come to this Buddha country. See this dreamlike country how beautiful it is, which was made by the teacher during a hundred thousand kalpas.

' "Look, the Buddha possessed of a mass of the best virtues shines, surrounded by Bodhisattvas. Endless is his splendour, and endless the light, and endless the life, and endless the assembly."

'And the lord Amitayus makes a smile of thirty-six niyutas of kotis of rays, which rays having issued from the circle of his mouth light up the thousand kotis of Buddha countries.

'And all these rays having returned there again settle on the head of the lord; gods and men perceive the delight, because they have seen there this light of him.

'There rises the Buddha-son, glorious, he in deed the mighty Avalokitesvara, and says: "What is the reason there, O Bhagavat, what is the cause, that thou smilest, O lord of the world?

' "Explain this, for thou knowest the sense, and art full of kind compassion, the deliverer of many living beings. All beings will be filled with joyful thoughts, when they have thus heard this excellent and delightful speech.

' "And the Bodhisattvas who have come from many worlds to Sukhavati in order to see the Buddha, having heard it and having perceived the great joy, will quickly inspect this country.

' "And beings come to this noble country, quickly obtain miraculous power, divine eye and divine ear, they remember their former births, and know the highest wisdom."

The Temple at Bodh Gaya, where Lord Buddha gained enlightenment

'Then Buddha Amitayus preaches: "This prayer was mine formerly, so that beings having in any way whatever heard my name should for ever go to my country.

' "And this my excellent prayer has been fulfilled, and beings having quickly come here from many worlds into my presence, never return from here, not even for one birth."

'If a Bodhisattva wishes here that his country should be such as this, and that he also should deliver many beings, through his name, through his preaching, and through his sight,

'Let him quickly and with speed go to the world Sukhavati, and having gone near Amitaprabha, let him worship a thousand kotis of Buddhas.

'Having worshipped many kotis of Buddhas, and having gone to many countries by means of their miraculous power, and having performed adoration in the presence of the Sugatas, they will go to Sukhavati with devotion.

'And again, O Ananda, there is a Bodhi-tree belonging to Amitayus, the Tathagata, holy and fully enlightened. That Bodhi-tree is ten hundred yojanas in height, having petals, leaves, and branches spread over eight hundred yojanas, having a circumference near the base of the root of five hundred yojanas, always in leaf, always in flower, always in fruit, of different colours, of many hundred thousand colours, of different leaves, of different flowers, of different fruits, adorned with many beautiful ornaments, shining with precious jewels, bright like the moon, beautified with precious jewels such as are fastened on Sakra's head, strewn with Chintamani jewels, well adorned with the best jewels of the sea, more than heavenly, hung with golden strings, adorned with hundreds of gold chains, jewel garlands, necklaces, bracelets, strings of red pearls and blue pearls, lion-twists (Simhalata), girdles, bunches, strings of jewels, and all kinds of jewels, covered with nets of bells, nets of all kinds of jewels, nets of pearls, and nets of gold, adorned with the emblems of the dolphin, the

Svastika, the Nandyavarta, and the moon, adorned with nets of jewels and of bells, and with ornaments of gold and of all kinds of jewels, in fact adorned according to the desires of beings whatever their wishes may be.

'And again, O Ananda, the sound and noise of that Bodhi-tree, when it is moved by the wind, reaches immeasurable worlds. And, O Ananda, for those beings whose hearing that Bodhi-tree reaches, no disease of the ear is to be feared until they reach Bodhi. And for those immeasurable, innumerable, inconceivable, incomparable, measureless, immense, and inexpressible beings, whose sight that Bodhi-tree reaches, no disease of the eye is to be feared until they reach Bodhi. And again, O Ananda, for those beings who smell the scent of that Bodhi-tree, no disease of the nose is to be feared until they reach Bodhi. For those beings who taste the fruits of that Bodhi-tree, no disease of the tongue is to be feared until they reach Bodhi. For those beings who are lighted up by the light of that Bodhi-tree, no disease of the body is to be feared until they reach Bodhi. And again, O Ananda, for those beings who meditate on that Bodhi-tree according to the Law, henceforward until they reach the Bodhi, no perplexity of their thought is to be feared. And all those beings, through the seeing of that Bodhi-tree, never turn away, namely, from the highest perfect knowledge. And they obtain three kinds of Kshanti or resignation, namely, Ghoshanuga, Anulomiki, resignation to natural consequences, and Anutpattika-dharma-kshanti, resignation to consequences which have not yet arisen, through the power of the former prayers of that same Tathagata Amitayus, through the service rendered by them to the former Jinas, and through the performance of the former prayers, to be well accomplished, and to be well conceived, without failure or without flaw.

'And again, O Ananda, those Bodhisattvas who have been born, are being born, or will be born there, are all bound to one birth only, and will thence indeed obtain the highest perfect knowledge; barring always the power of prayers, as in the case of those Bodhisattvas who are preaching with the voice of lions, who are girded with the noble armour of the Law, and who are devoted to the work of helping all people to attain Parinirvana.

'And again, O Ananda, in that Buddha country, those who are Sravakas are possessed of the light of a fathom, and those who are Bodhisattvas are possessed of the light of a hundred thousand kotis of yojanas; barring always the two Bodhisattvas, by whose light that world is everywhere shining with eternal splendour.'

Then the blessed Ananda said this to the Bhagavat: 'What are the names, O Bhagavat, of those two noble-minded Bodhisattvas?'

The Bhagavat said: 'One of them, O Ananda, is the noble-minded Bodhisattva Avalokitesvara, and the second is Mahasthamaprapta by name. And, O Ananda, these two were born there, having left this Buddha country here.

'And, O Ananda, those Bodhisattvas who have been born in that Buddha country are all endowed with the thirty-two marks of a great man, possessed of perfect members, skilled in meditation and wisdom, clever in all kinds of wisdom, having sharp organs, having well-restrained organs, having organs of sense capable of thorough knowledge, not mean, possessed of the five kinds of strength, of patience under censure, and of endless and boundless good qualities.

'And again, O Ananda, all those Bodhisattvas who have been born in that Buddha country are not deprived of the sight of Buddha, nor liable to fall down to the evil states. until they reach the Bodhi. Henceforward they all will never be forgetful of their former births barring always those who are devoted to their former place, during the disturbances of the kalpas, and while the five kinds of corruption prevail, when there is the appearance of blessed Buddhas in the world, as for instance, that of me at present.

'And again, O Ananda, all the Bodhisattvas who have been born in that Buddha country, having gone during one morning meal to the other world, worship many hundred thousand niyutas of kotis of Buddhas, as many as they like, through the favour of Buddha. They consider in many ways that they should worship Buddhas with such and such flowers, incense, lamps, scents, garlands, ointments, powder, cloaks, umbrellas, flags, banners, ensigns, music, concerts, and musical instruments; and, as soon as they have considered this, there arise also on their hands exactly such materials for every kind of worship. And while performing worship for those blessed Buddhas with those materials, beginning with flowers and ending with musical instruments, they lay up for themselves much immeasurable and innumerable merit. Again, if they wish that such handfullsof flowers should be produced on their hands, then such handfulls of heavenly flowers, of different colours, of many colours, of different scents, are produced on their hands as soon as thought of. They shower again and again such handfulls of flowers upon those blessed Buddhas. And the very smallest handfull of flowers, being thrown on high, appears above in the sky as an umbrella of flowers ten yojanas in circumference. And when the second has been thrown after it, the first does not fall down on the earth. There are handfulls of flowers there, which having been thrown up, appear in the sky as an umbrella of flowers twenty yojanas in circumference. There appear in the sky some flower-umbrellas, thirty, forty, or fifty yojanas in circumference, as far as a hundred thousand yojanas in circumference. Those Bodhisattvas there who perceive the noble pleasure and joy, and obtain the noble strength of thought, having caused a great and immeasurable and innumerable stock of good works to ripen, and having worshipped many hundred thousand niyutas of kotis of Buddhas, turn again to the world Sukhavati in one morning, through the favour of practising the former prayers of the same Tathagata Amitayus, owing to the hearing of the Law formerly given, owing to the stock of good works produced under former Jinas, owing to the perfect completion in the success of former prayers, owing to the well-ordered state of mind.

'And again, O Ananda, all those beings who have been born in that Buddha country recite the story of the Law, which is accompanied by omniscience. And for the beings in that Buddha country there exists no idea of property whatever. And all those going and walking through that Buddha country feel neither pleasure nor pain; stepping forward they have no desire, and with desire they do not step forward. They give no thought to any beings. And again, O Ananda, for those beings who have been born in that world Sukhavati, there is no idea of others, no idea of self, no idea of inequality, no strife, no dispute, no opposition. Full of equanimity, of benevolent thought, of tender thought, of affectionate thought, of useful thought, of serene thought, of firm thought, of unbiased thought, of undisturbed thought, of unagitated thought, of thought fixed on the practice of discipline and transcendent wisdom, having entered on knowledge which is a firm support to all thoughts, equal to the ocean in wisdom, equal to the mountain Meru in knowledge, rich in many good qualities, delighting in the music of the Bodhyangas, devoted to the music of Buddha, they discard the eye of flesh, and assume the heavenly eye. And having approached the eye of wisdom, having reached the eye of the Law, producing the eye of Buddha, showing it, lighting it, and fully exhibiting it, they attain perfect wisdom. And being bent on the equilibrium of the three elements, having subdued and calmed their thoughts, endowed with a perception of the causes of all things, clever in explanation of causes, endowed with the power of explaining the Law, or things such as they really are, clever in taking and refusing, clever in leading and not leading, clever in resting, they, being regardless of worldly stories, derive true pleasures from stories transcending the world. They are clever in examining all things, familiar with the knowledge of the cessation of the working of all things, perceiving even what cannot be seen, caring for nothing, attached to nothing, without cares, without pain, free without clinging to anything, free from impurity, of blameless behaviour, not clinging to anything, intent on the deep or profound laws,

Buddhist Chaitya at Karle, near Pune.

they do not sink, elevated to the entrance into the knowledge of Buddha difficult to comprehend, having obtained the path of one vehicle, free from doubt, beyond the reach of questionings, knowing the thoughts of others, free from self-confidence. Being elevated in knowledge, they are like the Sumeru; being imperturbable in thought, they are like the ocean; they surpass the light of the sun and moon, by the light of wisdom, and by the whiteness, brilliancy, purity, and beauty of their knowledge; by their light and splendour, they are like the colour of molten gold; by their patiently bearing the good and evil deeds of all beings, they are like the earth; by their cleaning and carrying off the taint of all sins, they are like water; by their burning the evil of pride in anything, they are like the king of fire; by not clinging to anything, they are like the wind; by pervading all things and yet not caring for anything, they are like the ether; by not being tainted by the whole world, they are like lotuses; by their shouting forth the Law, they are like the great cloud at the rainy season; by showering down the whole ocean of the Law, they are like the great rain; by overpowering great troops, they are like bulls; by the highest restraint of their thoughts, they are like great elephants; by being well trained, they are like noble horses; by their fearlessness, confidence, and heroism, they are like the lion, the king of beasts; by affording protection to all beings, they are like the Nyagrodha (fig-tree), the king of trees; by not being shaken by any calumniators, they are like the Sumeru, the king of mountains; by their feeling of unlimited love, they are like the sky; by their precedence, owing to their command of the Law, and their stock of all merit, they are like the great Brahman; by their not dwelling in what they have accumulated, they are like birds; by their scattering all calumniators, they are like Garuda, king of birds; by their not being averse to our obtaining difficult things, they are like the Udumbara flowers; calm like elephants, because their senses are neither crooked nor shaken; clever in decision, full of the sweet flavour of patience; without envy, because they do not hanker after the happiness of others; wise, because in their search after the Law, never tired of discussions on the Law; like the precious beryl, through their value; like jewel-mines, by their sacred knowledge; sweet-sounding by the noise of the great drum of the Law, striking the great kettle-drum of the Law, blowing the great trumpet-shell of the Law, raising the great banner of the Law, lighting the torch of the Law, looking for wisdom, not foolish, faultless, passionless, pure, refined, not greedy, fond of distributing, generous, open-handed, fond of distributing gifts, not stingy in giving instruction and food, not attached, without fear, without desires, wise, patient, energetic, bashful, orderly, fearless, full of knowledge, happy, pleasant to live with, obliging, enlightening the world, free from sorrow, free from taint, having left off the winking of the eye, possessing lightly acquired knowledge, strong in reasoning, strong in prayer, not crooked, not perverse; then, having accumulated a hundred thousand niyutas of kotis of lakshas of virtue, delivered from the thorns of pride, free from illusion, hatred, and passion; pure, devoted to what is pure, famous by the Jina-power, learned in the world, elevated by their purified knowledge, sons of the Jina, endowed with the vigour of thought, heroes, firm, unselfish, free from faults, unequalled, free from anger, collected, noble, heroes, bashful, energetic, possessed of memory, understanding, and prudence; sending forth the weapons of knowledge, possessed of purity, shining, free from faults and taints, endowed with memory, resting on serene knowledge. And such, O Ananda, are the beings in that Buddha country, stated briefly. But if the Tathagatas should describe them fully, even in a length of life that should last for a hundred thousand niyutas of kotis of kalpas, yet the end of the virtues of those good people would not be reached, and yet there would be no failure of the self-confidence of the Tathagata. And why? Because, O Ananda, both are indeed inconceivable and incomparable, first, the virtues of those Bodhisattvas, and secondly, the unsurpassed light of knowledge of the Tathagata.

'And now, O Ananda, stand up, facing westward, and having taken a handful of flowers, fall down. This is the quarter where that Bhagavat Amitabha, the Tathagata, holy and fully enlightened, dwells, remains, supports himself, and teaches the Law, whose spotless and pure name, famed in every quarter of the whole world with its ten quarters, the blessed Buddhas, equal to the grains of the sand of the river Ganga, speaking and answering again and again without stopping, extol, praise, and eulogize.'

After this, the blessed Ananda said this to the Bhagavat: 'I wish, O Bhagavat, to see that Amitabha, Amitaprabha, Amitayus, the Tathagata, holy and fully enlightened, and those noble-minded Bodhisattvas, who are possessed of a stock of merit amassed under many hundred thousand niyutas of kotis of Buddhas.'

At that moment this speech was spoken by the blessed Ananda, and immediately that Amitabha, the Tathagata, holy and fully enlightened, let such a ray of light go out of the palm of his own hand, that even the most distant Buddha country was shining with the great splendour. And again at that time, whatever black mountains, or jewel-mountains, or Merus, great Merus, Muchilindas, great Muchilindas, Chakravadas, great Chakravadas, or erections, or pillars, trees, woods, gardens, palaces, belonging to the gods and men, exist everywhere in hundred thousand kotis of Buddha countries; all these were pervaded and overcome by the light of that Tathagata. And as a man, followed by another at a distance of a fathom only, would see the other man, when the sun has risen, exactly in the same manner the Bhikshus, Bhikshunis, Upasakas, Upasikas, gods, Nagas, Yakshas, Rakshasas, Gandharvas, Asuras, Garudas, Kinnaras, Maharajas, men and not-men, in this Buddha country, saw at that time that Amitabha, the Tathagata, holy and fully enlightened, like the Sumeru, the king of mountains, elevated above all countries, surpassing all quarters, shining, warming, glittering, blazing; and they saw that great mass of Bodhisattvas, and that company of Bhikshus, by the grace of Buddha, from the pureness of that light. And as this great earth might be, when all covered with water, so that no trees, no mountains, no islands, no grasses, bushes, herbs, large trees, no rivers, chasms, waterfalls, would be seen, but only the one great earth which had all become an ocean, in exactly the same manner there is neither mark nor sign whatever to be seen in that Buddha country, except Sravakas, spreading their light over a fathom, and those Bodhisattvas, spreading their light over a hundred thousand kotis of yojanas. And that Bhagavat Amitabha, the Tathagata, holy and fully enlightened, overshadowing that mass of Sravakas and that mass of Bodhisattvas, is seen, illuminating all quarters. Again at that time all those Bodhisattvas, Sravakas, gods and men in that world Sukhavati, saw this world Saha and Sakyamuni, the Tathagata, holy and fully enlightened, surrounded by a holy company of Bhikshus, teaching the Law.

Then, the Bhagavat addressed the nobleminded Bodhisattva Ajita, and said: 'Do you see, O Ajita, the perfection of the array of ornaments and good qualities in that Buddha country; and above in the sky with charming parks, charming gardens, charming rivers and lotus lakes, scattered with many precious Padmas, Utpalas, Kumudas, and Pundarikas; and below, from the earth to the abode of the Akanishthas, the surface of the sky, covered with flowers, ornamented with wreaths of flowers, shining on the rows of many precious columns, frequented by flocks of all kinds of birds created by the Tathagata?'

The Bodhisattva Ajita said: 'I see, O Bhagavat.'

The Bhagavat said: 'Do you see again, O Ajita, those flocks of immortal birds, making the whole Buddha country resound with the voice of Buddha, so that those Bodhisattvas are never without meditating on Buddha?'

Ajita said: 'I see, O Bhagavat.'

The Bhagavat said: 'Do you see again, O Ajita, those beings, who have ascended to the palaces which extend over a hundred thousand yojanas in the sky, walking about respectfully?'

Ajita said: 'I see, O Bhagavat.'

The Bhagavat said: 'What do you think, O Ajita, is there any difference between the gods called Paranirmitavasavartins, and men in the world Sukhavati?'

Ajita said: 'I do not, O Bhagavat, perceive even one difference, so far as the men in that world of Sukhavati are endowed with great supernatural powers.'

The Bhagavat said: 'Do you see again, O Ajita, those men dwelling within the calyx of exce1lent lotus-flowers in that world Sukhavati?'

He said: 'As gods called Trayastrimsas or Yamas, having entered into palaces of fifty or hundred or five hundred yojanas in extent, are playing, sporting, walking about, exactly in the same manner I see, O Bhagavat, these men dwelling within the calyx of excellent lotus-flowers in the world Sukhavati.

'Again there are, O Bhagavat, beings who, being born miraculously, appear sitting cross-legged in the lotus-flowers. What is there, O Bhagavat, the cause, what the reason, that some dwell within the calyx, while others, being born miraculously, appear sitting cross-legged in the lotus-flowers?'

The Bhagavat said: 'Those Bodhisattvas, O Ajita, who, living in other Buddha countries, entertain doubt about being born in the world Sukhavati, and with that thought amass a stock of merit, for them there is the dwelling within the calyx. Those, on the contrary, who are filled with faith, and being free from doubt, amass a stock of merit in order to be born in the world Sukhavati, and conceive, believe, and trust in the perfect knowledge of the blessed Buddhas, they, being born miraculously, appear sitting cross-legged in the flowers of the lotus. And those noble-minded Bodhisattvas, O Ajita, who, living in other Buddha countries, raise theIr thought in order to see Amitabha,

Lord Buddha at Bagan, Myanmar

the Tathagata, holy and fully enlightened, who never entertain a doubt, believe in the perfect knowledge of Buddha and in their own stock of merit, for them, being born miraculously, and appearing cross-legged, there is, in one minute, such a body as that of other beings who have been born there long before. See, O Ajita, the excellent, immeasurable, unfailing, unlimited wisdom, that for their own benefit they are deprived during five hundred years of seeing Buddhas, seeing Bodhisattvas, hearing the Law, speaking about the Law with others, and thus collecting a stock of merit; they are indeed deprived of the successful attainment of every stock of merit, and that through their forming ideas tainted with doubt.

'And, O Ajita, there might be a dungeon belonging to an anointed Kshatriya king, inlaid entirely with gold and beryl, in which cushions, garlands, wreaths and strings are fixed, having canopies of different colours and kind, covered with silk cushions, scattered over with various flowers and blossoms, scented with excellent scents, adorned with arches, courts, windows, pinnacles, fire-places, and terraces, covered with nets of bells of the seven kinds of gems, having four angles, four pillars, four doors, four stairs; and the son of that king having been thrown into the dungeon for some misdeed is there, bound with a chain made of the Jambunada gold. And suppose there is a couch prepared for him, covered with many woollen cloths, spread over with cotton and feather cushions, having Kalinga coverings, and carpets, together with coverlids, red on both sides, beautiful and charming. There he might be then either sitting or resting. And there might be brought to him much food and drink, of various kinds, pure and well prepared. What do you think, O Ajita, would the enjoyment be great for that prince?'

Ajita said: 'Yes, it would be great, O Bhagavat.'

The Bhagavat said: 'What do you think, O Ajita, would he even taste it there, and notice it, or would he feel any satisfaction from it?'

He said: 'Not indeed, O Bhagavat; but on the contrary, when he had been led away by the king and thrown into the dungeon, he would only wish for deliverance from there. He would seek for the nobles, princes, ministers, women, elders, rich merchants, householders, and lords of castles, who might deliver him from that dungeon. Moreover, O Bhagavat, there is no pleasure for that prince in that dungeon, nor is he liberated, until the king shows him favour.'

The Bhagavat said: 'Thus, O Ajita, it is with those Bodhisattvas who, having fallen into doubt, amass a stock of merit, but doubt the knowledge of Buddha. They are born in that world Sukhavati, through the hearing of Buddha's name, and through the serenity of thought only; they do not, however, appear sitting cross-legged in the flowers of the lotus, being born miraculously, but dwell only in the calyx of the lotus-flowers. Moreover, for them there exist ideas of palaces and gardens. There is no discharge, there is no phlegm or mucus, there is nothing disagreeable to the mind. But they are deprived of seeing Buddhas, hearing the Law, seeing Bodhisattvas, speaking about and ascertaining the Law, gathering any new stock of merit, and practising the Law, during five hundred years. Moreover, they do not rejoice there or perceive satisfaction. But they wish to remove one another, and then they step out behind. And it is not known whether their exit takes place above, below, or across. See, O Ajita, there might be worshippings of many hundred thousand niyutas of kotis of Buddhas during those five hundred years, and also many, immense, innumerable, immeasurable stocks of merit to be amassed. But all this they destroy by the fault of doubt. See, O Ajita, to how great an injury the doubt of the Bodhisattvas leads. Therefore now, O Ajita, after the Bodhisattvas without doubting have quickly raised their thoughts towards the Bodhi, in order to obtain power of conferring happiness for the benefit of all creatures, their stock of merit should be turned towards their being born in the world Sukhavati, where the blessed Amitabha, the Tathagata, holy and fully enlightened, dwells.'

After these words, the Bodhisattva Ajita thus spoke to the Bhagavat: 'O Bhagavat, will the Bodhisattvas, who have gone away from this Buddha country, or from the side of other blessed Buddhas, be born in the world Sukhavati?'

The Bhagavat said: 'Indeed, O Ajita, seventy-two niyutas of kotis of Bodhisattvas are gone away from this Buddha country, who will be born in the world Sukhavati; Bodhisattvas, who will never return, thanks to the stock of merit, which they have accumulated under many hundred thousand niyutas of kotis of Buddhas. What then shall be said of those with smaller stocks of merit? 1. Eighteen hundred niyutas of kotis of Bodhisattvas will be born in the world Sukhavati from the place of the Tathagata Dushprasaha. 2. There lives in the Eastern quarter the Tathagata named Ratnakara. From his place ninety kotis of Bodhisattvas will be born in the world Sukhavati. 3. Twenty-two kotis of Bodhisattvas will be born in the world Sukhavati from the place of the Tathagata Jyotishprabha. 4. Twenty-five kotis of Bodhisattvas will be born in the world Sukhavati from the place of the Tathagata Amitaprabha. 5. Sixty kotis of Bodhisattvas will be born in the world Sukhavati from the place of the Tathagata Lokapradipa. 6. Sixty-four kotis of Bodhisattvas will be born in the world Sukhavati from the place of the Tathagata Nagabhibhu. 7. Twenty-five kotis of Bodhisattvas will be born in the world Sukhavati from the place of the Tathagata Virajsahprabha. 8. Sixteen kotis of Bodhisattvas will be born in the world Sukhavati from the place of the Tathagata Simha. 9. Eighteen thousand Bodhisattvas will be born in the world Sukhavati from the place of the Tathagata Deva. 10. Eighty-one niyutas of kotis of Bodhisattvas will be born in the world Sukhavati from the place of the Tathagata Sriketa. I I. Ten niyutas of kotis of Bodhisattvas will be born in the world Sukhavati from the place of the Tathagata Narendraraja. 12. Twelve thousand Bodhisattvas will be born in the world Sukhavati from the place of the Tathagata Balabhijna. 13. Twenty-five kotis of

Bodhisattvas, who have obtained strength, having gone to one place in one week of eight days, and having turned to the West during ninety hundred thousand niyutas of kotis of kalpas, will be born in the world Sukhavati from the place of the Tathagata Pushpadhvaja. 14. Twelve kotis of Bodhisattvas will be born in the world Sukhavati from the place of the Tathagata Jvalanadhipati. I5. From the place of the Tathagata Vaisaradyaprapta, sixty-nine kotis of Bodhisattvas will be born in the world Sukhavati, in order to see the Tathagata Amitabha, to bow before him, to worship him, to ask questions of him, and to consult him. For this reason, O Ajita, I might proclaim during a full niyuta of kotis of kalpas the names of those Tathagatas, from whom the Bodhisattvas proceed in order to see that Tathagata Amitabha in the world Sukhavati, to bow before him, and to worship him, and yet the end could not be reached.

'See, O Ajita, what easy gains are gained by those beings who will hear the name of the Tathagata Amitabha, holy and fully enlightened. Nor will those beings be of little faith, who will obtain at least onc joyful thought of that Tathagata and of this treatise of the Law. Therefore now, O Ajita, I invite you, and command you to proclaim this treatise of the Law, before the world together with the gods. Having plunged into the vast universe full of fire, no one ought to turn back, if he has but once conceived the thought of going across. And why? Because kotis of Bodhisattvas indeed, O Ajita, return from the highest perfect knowledge, on account of not hearing such treatises of the Law as this. Therefore, from a wish for this treatise of the Law, a great effort should be made to hear, learn, and remember it, and to study it for the sake of fully grasping it and widely making it known. A good copy of it should be kept, after it has been copied in a book, if only during one night and day, or even during the time necessary for milking a cow. The name of Master should be given to a teacher who desires to conduct quickly innumerable beings to the state of never returning from the highest perfect knowledge, namely, in order that they may see the Buddha country of that blessed Amitabha, the Tathagata, and to acquire the excellent perfection of the array of good qualities peculiar to his own Buddha country.

'And, O Ajita, such beings will have easily gained their gains who, having amassed a stock of merit, having performed service under former Jinas, and having been guided by Buddhas, shall hear in future, until the destruction of the good Law, such-like excellent treatises of the Law, treatises which are praised, eulogized, and approved of by all Buddhas, and convey quickly the great knowledge of omniscience. And those also who, when they have heard it, shall obtain excellent delight and pleasure, and will learn, retain, recite and grasp, and wisely preach it to others, and be delighted by its study, or, having copied it at least, will worship it, will certainly produce much good work, so that it is difficult to count it.

'Thus indeed, O Ajita, I have done what a Tathagata ought to do. It is now for you to devote yourself to it without any doubt. Do not doubt the perfect and unfailing knowledge of Buddha. Do not enter into the dungeon made of gems built up in every way. For indeed, the birth of a Buddha, O Ajita, is difficult to be met with, so is the instruction in the Law, and also a timely birth. O Ajita, the way to gain the perfection, Paramita of all stocks of merit has been proclaimed by me. Do now exert yourselves and move forward. O Ajita, I grant indeed a great favour to this treatise ot the Law. Be valiant so that the laws of Buddhas may not perish or disappear. Do not break the command of the Tathagata.'

'Then at that time, the Bhagavat spoke these verses:

'Such hearings of me will not be for people who have not done good; but those who are heroes and perfect, they will hear this speech.

'And those by whom the Lord of the world, the enlightened and the light-giver, has been seen, and the law been heard reverentially, will obtain the highest joy.

Lord Buddha, Polannaruva

'Low people of slothful minds cannot find any delight in the laws of Buddha; those who have worshipped in the Buddha countries learn the service of the Lords of the three worlds.

'As a blind man in darkness does not know the way, and much less can show it, so also he who is only a Sravaka in the knowledge of Buddha; how then should beings who are ignorant!

'The Buddha only knows the virtues of a Buddha; but not gods, Nagas, Asuras, Yakshas, and Sravakas; even for Anekabuddhas, there is no such way, as when the knowledge of a Buddha is being manifested.

'If all beings had attained bliss, knowing the highest meaning in pure wisdom, they would not in kotis of kalpas or even in a longer time tell all the virtues of one Buddha.

'Thereupon they would attain Nirvana, preaching for many kotis of kalpas, and yet the measure of the knowledge of a Buddha would not be reached, for such is the wonderfulness of the knowledge of the Jinas.

'Therefore, a learned man of an intelligent race who believes my words, after having perceived all paths of the knowledge of the Jinas, should utter speech, saying, "Buddha is wise."

'Now and then a man is found, now and then a Buddha appears, knowledge of the object of faith is acquired after a long time,—therefore, one should strive to acquire the knowledge of the object of faith.'

And while this treatise of the Law was being delivered, twelve kotis of niyutas of beings obtained the pure and spotless eye of the Law with regard to Laws. Twenty-four hundred thousand niyutas of kotis of beings obtained the Anagamin reward. Eight hundred Bhikshus had their thoughts delivered from faults so as to cling no more to anything. Twenty-five kotis of Bodhisattvas obtained resignation to things to come. And by forty hundred thousand niyutas of kotis of the human and divine race,

Lord Buddha, Srilanka

thoughts such as had never risen before were turned toward the highest perfect knowledge, and their stocks of merit were made to grow toward their being born in the world Sukhavati, from a desire to see the Tathagata, the blessed Amitabha. And all of them having been born there, will in proper order be born in other worlds, as Tathagatas, called Manjusvara, sweet-voiced. And eighty kotis of niyutas having acquired resignation under the Tathagata Dipankara, never turning back again from the highest perfect knowledge, rendered perfect by the Tathagata Amitayus, practising the duties of former Bodhisattvas, will carry out, after they are born in the world Sukhavati, the duties enjoined in the former Pranidhanas, prayers.

At that time this universe, the three millions of worlds, trembled in six ways. And various miracles were seen. On earth everything was perfect, and human and divine instruments were played, and the shout of joy was heard as far as the world of the Akanishthas.

Thus spoke the Bhagavat enraptured, and the noble-minded Bodhisattva Ajita, and the blessed Ananda, the whole Assembly, and the world, with gods, men, spirits, mighty birds, and fairies, applauded the speech of the Bhagavat.

The praise of the beauty of the excellences of Sukhavati, the country of the blessed Amitabha, the Tathagata, the entry of the Bodhisattva on the stage of 'never returning', the story of Amitabha, the Mahayana sutra of the Description of Sukhavati is finished.

• • •